IN IT TO

# WIN IT

*THE WORLD'S LEADING EXPERTS*
REVEAL THEIR TOP

## STRATEGIES FOR

# WINNING

*in*

## BUSINESS & LIFE

Published by CelebrityPress™, Orlando, FL
A division of The Celebrity Branding Agency®

Celebrity Branding® is a registered trademark
Printed in the United States of America.

ISBN: 9780985364335
LCCN: 2012936236

Most CelebrityPress™ titles are available at special quantity discounts for bulk purchases for sales promotions, premiums, fundraising, and educational use. Special versions or book excerpts can also be created to fit specific needs.

For more information, please write:

CelebrityPress™
520 N. Orlando Ave, #2
Winter Park, FL 32789
or call 1.877.261.4930

Visit us online at www.CelebrityPressPublishing.com

IN IT TO

# WIN IT

THE WORLD'S LEADING EXPERTS
REVEAL THEIR TOP

## STRATEGIES FOR

# WINNING

*in*

## BUSINESS & LIFE

# Contents

# Foreword

## By Tom Hopkins

*In It to Win It!* I love this title. And so do each of the other authors in this book. It has inspired all of us to write something we hope will touch your heart, inspire your mind and help you take the steps necessary to achieve the success of your dreams.

If you don't have passion for your life's work, why even waste your time and effort being involved with it? If you're going to do anything—small or large—why not do it to the best of your ability? Life is way too short not to enjoy what you do or not to do something that you enjoy.

Do you think any Olympic athletes have ever trained with the image in their minds of winning the bronze medal? Of course not. They all picture themselves on that top step and hearing their country's national anthem played over the speaker system. The same goes for Grammy winners, winners of Academy Awards, the Emmys and even your top local marathon runners and high school athletes. They bring their best to whatever they're working on every single day.

This enthusiasm for triumph doesn't apply just to actors and athletes. It applies to everyone—in every walk of life. Parents aspire to successfully raise intelligent, responsible children. Employers strive to build solid companies that will support not only them, but also the families of the employees who make it great.

It doesn't matter what you do as much as it matters how well you do it. Even taxi drivers and refuse workers know when they're doing the best they can at their jobs.

I once met a man who had worked his entire adult life in a tollbooth on the highway. I was being driven to the airport. The tollbooth worker greeted my driver with a smile and an enthusiastic "Good morning, sir! Thank you, sir. And, you have a wonderful day!" He then leaned out of his booth and said to me, "And you sir, I hope you have a beautiful day as well." I could tell this level of enthusiasm was not a random act. It was a habit this man had developed. I had my driver pull over to the side of the road and made my way back to the tollbooth. Being a speaker on self-development and sales training, I knew I had to talk with this guy!

He saw me coming and asked what he could do for me. I asked, "How long have you been doing this job?" His reply was, "Seventeen years, sir." I was baffled and said, "Let me get this right, you have stood here in this little booth all day long for 17 years in all kinds of weather. Why are you so happy?" His reply was perfect. "I've got it made! I'm only here 7 hours a day. At home I have a wonderful wife and beautiful children. On the weekends, we have an RV that allows us to enjoy traveling. My pension is not bad. Our home will be paid for by the time I retire. I've got it made!"

Was that man successful? Absolutely! He had goals for his life and was achieving them. Was he in it to win it? You bet. He showed up every day…and with an attitude that made not only his day but also the day of everyone he encountered.

Whatever success and happiness means to you, go after it with passion and enthusiasm and you'll be bound to win. You, too, will be IN IT TO WIN IT!

# CHAPTER 1

# Everyone Is In Sales

## By Tom Hopkins

As a public speaker and sales trainer, I have taught millions of career professionals how to effectively sell their products and services. But, more importantly, I have helped them understand that they must sell themselves first. And that's a lesson I would like to share with everyone on the planet.

Everyone is in sales. You may not want to believe me because you think "selling" is a nasty word or dishonorable profession. Perhaps you've had a bad past experience with a salesperson who matches Hollywood's description of the stereotype—pushy, manipulative and slick. All I can say to that is, please don't pre-judge this topic. Understanding it can mean the difference between spending the rest of your life living in mediocrity, or living the successful life of your dreams.

Whether you like the term or not, you are involved in selling. You start selling the moment you open your eyes in the morning. That's what self-motivation really is. You sell yourself on getting out of bed on time. Completing just that one simple activity can make or break your day.

You sell yourself on saving money, exercising, eating properly and doing all those things that you know will make you a better you, help you to live a longer and healthier life. The most important sale you will ever make is the one you make to the person in the mirror. Once you believe in yourself, anything is possible.

Before you go out to sell yourself to others, though, you have to do what every professional salesperson does—prepare. The amount of care you give to grooming and dressing will impact your attitude for the day. If you don't believe me, think about how much mental damage a noticeable shaving nick, badly broken nail or even a bad hair day can make on your attitude. Realizing part way into your day that you have a stain on your shirt or un-shined shoes doesn't do much for your confidence, does it? It negatively impacts your ability and desire to sell yourself.

It's human nature to judge others. We're sizing ourselves up in comparison to the other guy or gal all the time. Because of that, things like broken nails and stained shirts matter. It's like we're all playing a game with points. You lose points on bad hair days and gain them when your shoes are shined. When interacting with others, you want to keep your points on par with or higher than theirs if you want them to "buy" you. People like to do business with, or hang out with, people who are like them.

You wouldn't try to join a group that was way out of your comfort zone unless you really needed to, would you? Of course not. Where comfort is lacking, credibility falters and successful persuasion is hard to come by. But, if you wanted to get the folks in that group to like you, for whatever reason, you would try to be like them. You might read the same magazines, dress like them or purchase items common to the folks in that group.

You may not realize it, but every little thing about you that lacks perfection in whatever you endeavor, however you personally define it, is like having a small dart of negativity hit you. Add up a bunch of those darts throughout the day and you will feel emotionally drained. That could easily lead to being distracted, negative, unproductive or even immobilized. Any of those things could prevent you from putting your best self forward.

I'm not saying that a broken nail by itself will ruin your day, though for some people it could. What I'm saying is that the cumulative effect of inattention to the simple details that could make your day great, might keep you from being successful at selling yourself to the world. If you're not having much success in getting what you want out of life, take a glance in the mirror. Would you buy whatever it is you're selling from that person? If not, give serious consideration to making some changes in how you present yourself to others.

So, who do you sell to besides yourself?

If you're in a relationship, you sell yourself to your spouse or significant other. You want them to "buy" the value of the bonds you have created every day, not just on the day you get married. People who fail to continue selling themselves to the other in relationships often bring about the end of those relationships.

If you have children in your life, you sell those kids on everything – from your values to doing well in school to eating healthy foods and picking up their toys. That is, unless you're one of those domineering parents who get things done through fear. Please note that when that's the case, as soon as those kids get out from under your watchful eye, they will not likely continue to "own" your values because you didn't ever sell them.

You sell extended family members on get-togethers. You persuade them as to where to meet. You suggest what food to share and recommend how to spend that allotted time. You also sell those folks on sharing the responsibilities of caring for fellow family members in need. If you've ever been in this situation, you will know that demanding or "guilting" people into helping just isn't the way to succeed in the long run. You have to persuade them that it's a wise decision to make.

You sell your employer on your level of skill and competence. If you are unemployed, you better be working on selling yourself into a job.

You sell your co-workers on your character and your dependability. When they "buy" you (it's spelled "trust"), the work gets done quickly and efficiently. In some cases, you get promoted by selling others on following you as a leader.

You sell your friends on where to have lunch, what movies to see, books to read, or recipes to try. In these instances, the word "sell" might be substituted with the word "recommend" but it still means selling.

If you are in business, you may also sell a product or service. At the very least, you sell your company's clients on how professional and competent your entire team is.

Every person on the staff of a business is in sales. Even if you work in the warehouse, packing boxes for shipment, the quality of your work makes an impact on the client on the receiving end. You may never meet them in person, but you are selling them on the company's ability to serve their needs well.

If you're not sure how that is selling, consider the following questions: What do clients think about the company when their package arrives with something that is not what they ordered? How about when the product inside the box is damaged because it wasn't padded well? Do you think they'll consider ordering from your company again? Do you think their decision might impact the bottom line? Do you think the impact on the bottom line might affect your ability to get a raise? Or, worse, do you think your quality of work affects whether or not you get to keep your job? Of course it does. Every person on the staff of a business is in sales.

The people who answer the phones for a business are in sales. They are the initial point of contact between the business and the client. If they represent the company well with a cheerful voice, professional demeanor and do their job correctly, the client's perception of the company increases. If they answer gruffly or as if they're distracted, how important does that customer feel?

You are in sales for whatever company you work with and no matter what your title is.

When your title is business owner, sales associate or customer service person, it's your direct responsibility to serve the needs of the people who will trade you their money for your goods. However, before anyone gets to enjoy the benefits of your skill at selling the product, they need to buy you. Theodore Roosevelt is known to have said, "Nobody cares how much you know, until they know how much you care." You have to sell yourself first.

If you represent a product or service that requires the client to purchase repeatedly, they really have to like you. They are not just looking at the advantages of your product. They are wondering if they want to have you in their lives every week, month, six months or whatever. It's not uncommon for long-term clients to contact companies asking for a different representative to serve their account when they don't like the person, but love the product. The company then has to choose between keeping that salesperson on the account and keeping the account. The decision will most likely be made in favor of the bottom line.

So, being likeable is critical to selling. If people don't like you, they won't want anything from you, not even your opinion on the weather. To be likeable, you must be comfortable smiling, greeting others with warmth and exuding empathy for them while putting yourself forth as a positive image for your company.

Going back to dress and grooming, as a true sales representative do you represent your company well? If you sell hair care products and you are in need of a fresh cut and style, how effective do you think you'll be? On the other hand, if you look like a class act, potential clients will assume that your company is one, too.

Not only must you represent your company well by sight, but so should whatever you bring with you to meetings with clients. This includes your computer, brief case or tote, and any visual aids. Your materials must be clean, neat and well organized.

If you lack organization during your presentation with clients, what will they think about how you'll handle their business? They'll think you'll forget details, that there may be errors in the paperwork and so on. If they are concerned about your ability to serve their needs, it may not matter how good your product or service is. Your lack of organization just created a wall of sales resistance that you may never be able to scale or break through.

So, how do you sell yourself other than making a good first impression by being well groomed and organized?

You must be punctual. Better to be 20 minutes early to a meeting than 2 minutes late. If you're meeting someone in a part of town you've never been to before, don't just rely on Google™ maps. Call ahead and ask for landmarks or if there is any construction in the area that might lengthen your arrival over the ETA given on the map website. Being late is a rough way to start any kind of relationship. Even if the world stopped for those two minutes, causing you to be late, the impression will be that you didn't care enough to be on time—that something else was more important.

To sell well, your first goals are to help people to like you, trust you and want to listen to you. You do that by being better than they expect, and by making them feel important. This applies both to business and personal situations.

In traditional selling, you also have to get the dollar signs out of your eyes. Have you ever been approached by a salesperson who emanated greed? Despite the best efforts of myself and hundreds of other sales trainers on the planet, they're still out there. They do not come across with a professional air of service. Rather you feel they're trying to suck the money right out of your wallet before you even glance at the product. Creepy, isn't it? If you really want to sell someone a product, service or an idea, you must approach them with their own interests at heart. What benefit is it to the other person to give you their valuable time and attention? Or to do whatever it is you're asking of them?

There's an old sales strategy that uses something similar to a radio station call letters. It's WII-FM. Those letters stand for "What's In It For Me?" Before you try to persuade anyone to do anything, buy anything or go anywhere, you must answer that question from THEIR perspective. What's in it for them? That's where you begin.

You see, selling isn't about you. You are just the matchmaker putting ideas and products together with people. You are opening up the minds and hearts of people to the benefits of what you or your product has to offer them. You are helping them to discover if they have a need for those benefits and then to rationalize making a commitment of their time or their money (in some cases both).

It's the same strategy for getting people to volunteer for the Neighborhood Watch program as it is to sell them the latest technological gadget. The great leaders of history were great salespeople. They presented situations and excited potential followers about the benefits to be gained by joining forces with them—sometimes to the death. Yet those people went gladly because they believed they would be better off following than staying where they were.

And how are ideas and products presented for sale? People who are very good at selling never push with facts. They pull by asking questions. Those questions are crafted specifically to capture the interest of the potential buyer and build their curiosity to know more. Rather than stating that your product is the best that ever was, you would be wise to ask the other party what they thought of a product that was the best. Ask about their experience with products such as yours. Ask what they liked, disliked or would change about that product. If you ask the right questions, they'll tell you exactly where their interests lie. They'll tell you what they want to own, change or will accept. If what you are offering is a good match, then you have an obligation to share your knowledge with them.

Everyone is in sales. Think about the next situation where you hope to persuade, sway, motivate or influence the outcome in your favor. Even if it's just where to have dinner tonight, it's a selling situation. Rather than approach it reflexively, give the situation a bit of thought; prepare and sell the other parties on agreeing with you. Once you realize how easy it is to succeed in sales—with some thought and preparation— you'll think differently about every presentation no matter how small, and handle it in such a manner as to achieve greater success. You'll be **In It to Win It**!

## About Tom

Tom Hopkins is world-renowned as a master at helping sales and business professionals learn the communication skills necessary to educate clients and assist them in making wise buying decisions. Tom's primary focus is to eliminate the stereotype of the pushy, unscrupulous salesperson portrayed on television and in the movies.

Tom wasn't born to wealth and privilege. In fact, he wasn't always successful. An average student, he started his working career in construction, working on the old Dodger stadium. The hours were long. The work was grueling especially in the heat of the summer. Married and with a child on the way, he knew there had to be a better way to earn a decent income for his young family.

In his early twenties Tom entered the field of real estate. He failed miserably his first six months in the business. After all, his only suit was a band uniform he had from high school and his only mode of transportation was a motorcycle. To top that off, even though he was 20, he looked like he was closer to age 15. Clients would come into the real estate office and upon seeing him, ask if his dad was in.

After observing what the more successful real estate agents were doing, he started a learning process that involved selling skills, psychology, time management, and self-development. By the age of 27, he had achieved millionaire status through the use of his selling skills – helping 1,153 families with the great American dream of home ownership.

Upon achieving such great success, Tom was often asked to speak. The talks he gave about what he did and said with clients developed into the legendary sales training programs he has offered since 1976. Tom teaches selling fundamentals—the foundational training upon which millions of successful careers have been built at live events, through video and audio recordings and in the 14 books he has authored. His strategies and tactics have proven successful in a wide range of industries and through all sorts of economic cycles.

Tom's books include the million-plus-selling *"How to Master the Art of SellSelling,"* the award-winning *"Selling in Tough Times," "Selling for Dummies™," "Low Profile Selling"* and *"Sell It Today, Sell It Now,"* which was co-authored with Pat Leiby and *"The Certifiable Salesperson"* co-authored with Laura Laaman, as well as industry-specific tomes for the real estate and financial services markets.

Selling is Tom's hobby and his passion. His goal is to shorten the learning curve of those who choose it as a career. He makes selling easy to comprehend. His teaching style is entertaining and memorable.

Tom Hopkins understands both sides of the selling equation. He appreciates the fears of both buyers and salespeople. Buyers don't want to be "sold" anything. Salespeople fear failure. The selling skills and strategies that Tom Hopkins teaches reflect an understanding of how to communicate with buyers so they feel confident in making wise buying decisions.

Tom Hopkins International, Inc.
7531 East Second Street
Scottsdale, Arizona USA 85251
www.tomhopkins.com
info@tomhopkins.com
480-949-0786
800-528-0446
Twitter: @TomHopkinsSales
LinkedIn: /TomHopkinsSalesTrainer

# CHAPTER 2

# TRANSFORM YOUR SALES AND BUSINESS: THINK LIKE AN OWNER

## By Bob Sbraccia

If you are a sales professional or a business owner, you know the importance of delivering on your financial objectives. The best way to transform a sales team or to catapult your individual career path into superstardom is to **Think Like an Owner**. This is a paradigm shift and can be met with resistance from a lot of folks, both sales reps and sales managers alike. The "good *employee*" who *processes* internal business operations often looks and thinks much differently than the "good employee" who *generates* revenue. The later *creates*, while the former *processes* work created by others. Both types of employees are needed and valuable; however, creating sales requires a different mindset. In addition to the specialized requisite skills of customer-facing account executives, the biggest differentiator in successful sales cultures is the conscious shift from *reactionary employees* to *proactive, entrepreneurial employees* who attack challenges like vested business owners. In my years of local, regional, and national sales and sales management experience, I've found that the executives who approach their job as if they were a franchise *owner* are consistently in the top 10% of their profession. I've also identified five core principles of successful business *ownership*.

Understand and master them to achieve highly-differentiated sales re-sults, an accelerated career path, or to transform your company's culture.

## THE 5 PRINCIPLES OF BUSINESS OWNERSHIP

1. Take Accountability

2. Know Your Business

3. Formulate Your Own Sales Plan – And Execute

4. Communicate a Compelling Value Proposition

5. Don't Settle for Trading Time for Money...Trade Results for (More) Money Instead

### *1. Take Accountability*

If you ever want to know what a company's priorities are, you only have to look as far as the sales compensation plan. If you roll up that comp plan, and put it up to your ear like you might a seashell you find on the beach, you won't hear the sound of the ocean. But you will hear the voice of ownership, loud and clear, proclaiming the financial objec-tives and assigning the monetary value on achieving them. And so that there's no confusion, you should also hear that **you are 100% account-able** for producing the financial objectives. Whether you are the Vice President of Sales, Regional Sales Director, frontline Sales Manager, or an individual sales contributor – you, and every member of your team - are each 100% accountable. Whether it's dollars, market share, share change, or units – whatever the metric (and there may be more than one) - it's better to embrace this accountability and confidently go about your business. When this epiphany occurs, then the remaining four steps to your transformation to an Owner's Mindset can fall into place. The good *employee* who processes work tends to avoid accountability and clings to the comfortable. The *business owner* accepts accountability to be a catalyst for growth. You can have growth. You can have comfort. But you can't have both at the same time. Take your decision wisely.

### *2. Know Your Business*

There is no substitute for knowing your business. *Owners* invest the time to know and understand the business drivers and forces that impact their business, industry, market – right down to their individual custom-ers. Dedicate time to build relationships and talk to key thought leaders. Continually work on becoming a technical expert and valuable resource to your customers. Be externally focused on the customer and discover the customer's pain points and identify areas of opportunity. Internally, be a willing and valuable collaborator across cross-functional teams. Once you identify the main business drivers and the relationships at play within market events and networks of influence, then you can establish a clear line of vision to your finish line: your financial targets. The person who knows how to do a task well will always have a job . . . But the person who knows *why* will always be the boss.

### 3. Formulate Your Own Sales Plan – And Execute

What paths will lead to success and what paths will lead to heartache? First, I've found that setting targets 30%-40% above the company's quota is the first step in any successful plan. If you plan only to achieve 100%, you leave zero room for error. Sorry, but that's just plain old bad *employee* planning. If you plan for 110%, you only have 10% margin for error. Would you stake your business (or your job) on such a small margin error? Knowing your business intimately will give you the ability to balance your stretch goals with attainability. Once the realistic stretch goals are defined, then work backwards. Who are the must-win customers? Analyze your sales data, (unit sales, average selling price, price increase pull-through, new products, etc.), and set account-specific plans to identify sales contributions to your plan. Allocate your budget and limited resources to those strategic accounts that make the plan. Understand that focusing resources on your must-win customers in the first six to nine months of the year gives you the best chance to yield same-year results. I typically plan to use 67% - 75% of my annual budget in the first half of the year because 4th quarter seeds aren't typically harvested until the next year. Execute and spend purposefully to shorten sales cycles and pop those must-win customers early. Monitor each strategy and tactic for effectiveness and be prepared to make in-flight adjustments to correct your course as needed.

Here's one of my favorite tips - share your plan with your management team. Invite their inspection and help. Give your manager a blue print on how to assist you in ways you know will drive your business. *Employees* tent to be fearful of goals and avoid them – mostly because of trust. They don't trust that they can control their results and they also don't trust that their managers won't use the plan against them as a whip. *Owners*, on the other hand, embrace challenge and work with other stakeholders to achieve common goals. I've had some of my best years in business when I missed every stretch goal I set for myself, yet outpaced national benchmarks by double digits. Earning the respect of my colleagues and management team was even more valuable. Having the right plan in place means never having to say you're sorry.

### 4. Communicate a Compelling Value Proposition

So how do you *sell* your product or service to targeted customers? In other words, what makes them *buy*? I've found the least effective sales technique is the data dump. That's when you take a really deep breath and in a single, prolonged exhale, dump the entire list of product features learned in training with an obligatory (and premature) feeble attempt at a close. The data dump shuts down the customer. The better approach is to build the business case with a compelling value proposition that calculates all the impacts to the customer's business – both tangible and intangible. But it doesn't stop there. A truly effective value proposition keeps the client engaged and sells **over** the competition by measuring the marginal impact of your product or solution. It focuses on the impact (of the benefit) and not the feature. Qualify and quantify the impacts your solutions offer, and provide the 'so what' for the buyer. Exactly how to construct your unique value proposition is beyond the scope of this chapter; however, you can check out marketing for minimally invasive surgical procedures, CRMs, cloud computing solutions, and online college degree programs for some good examples of building successful value propositions. Take the fear out of closing, and increase your closing rate with a well-crafted value proposition.

### 5. Don't Settle for Trading Time for Money…Trade Results for (More) Money Instead

Predictably, sales compensation is linked to those accomplishments that add the most value to the company. If you're in the sales game and you want to have a banner year, align your priorities with the comp plan, but there's one caveat: don't confuse 'activity' with 'productivity'. *Owners* only want to pay for results, not busywork. The most successful owners don't dole out average pay for average results; rather, they offer remarkable income for remarkable results. When a sales rep thinks like an *employee*, he or she has decided to trade time for money. When you start to focus on activity-based metrics like number of calls per day, you bear the shackles of an *employee* trading time for money.

In dashboard sales management cultures, there is no value assigned for quality – there's just quantity. And in these cultures, reps learn quickly not to be an 'outlier.' Results are buried in the pile of ineffective activity and you hear phrases like 'playing the sales game.' Sadly, some companies enable their sales team to be time-traders. It is an easy existence at first. Reps have complete control over delivering the requisite activity metrics like call reach and frequency. For the time being, everybody's comfortable. Over time, however, as sales plateau, new products are launched, or market events create opportunities or threats, sales reps (and their companies) find themselves in a bind. *How do I create more customers? How can I increase share? How can I increase revenue? How much* share and *how much* revenue? *How can I capitalize on an unpredicted market event?* When you begin to ask these questions, you have turned the corner to thinking like an owner. You will throw away meaningless *check-the-box* activities and put a laser focus on those high-value, high-priority activities that will impact your business and catapult you to sales success. Making the paradigm shift from an *employee* mindset to an *owner's* mindset puts the focus where it should be - on results. When you realize it is more rewarding to trade results for money, you will never want to go back to trading your time for money again. And when sales organizations empower their sales reps to drive business as if they were *territory franchise owners*, then true transformation can occur. Healthy sales cultures recognize great effort with words of praise and encouragement, but reserve financial reward for great results.

## A PERSONAL REAL-LIFE CASE STUDY

We've all heard it said that, "Knowledge is Power." And, in my formative years, I truly believed it. As a Regional Manager, a new understanding had evolved. I learned that in business, knowledge isn't power . . . But the expert application of knowledge is! Perhaps the best examples of where I leveraged the 5 principles of ownership were in the medical device sales and the pharmaceutical sales professions.

In these industries, it was not uncommon to throw bodies at a problem. When drug companies wanted more sales, they typically hired more sales people. New product? Hire more salespeople. Create a product specialty sales position? Hire more salespeople. To further ensure that their products got sufficient share of voice, pharmaceutical companies commonly deployed multiple sales reps in teams called 'clusters' or 'pods' to cover the same territory and call on the same doctors. When a sales cluster of three sales reps owned a sales territory, it often translated into **no one** owning it because individual accountability was diluted and murky. Decisions by committee followed as part of the culture. Diagnostic tools like weekly activity reports and managers' dashboards became misinterpreted for real fee-for-performance measures of sales success. Sales management emphasized the importance of activity metrics like reach and frequency, as if the sales calls were just one of many impressions on a highway billboard or an online ad on Google. But by making the activity metric itself the point of emphasis, the unintentional consequence *was the de-emphasis of the sales outcome.* As a result, growth waned and so did job satisfaction.

I once asked a sales colleague *"How was your day?"*

He responded rather proudly, *"Great! I got in 10 sales calls by lunchtime."*

*"Great!"* I said. *"How much new business do you expect?"*

*"None, really,"* replied the sales *employee*, *"but I got my call average up!"*

*Really?!!!* Making sales calls based on convenience instead of meaningful business outcomes? Whether you subscribed to this practice or not (and not everybody did – I've had the pleasure to work with some very talented Device and Pharma sales reps), nobody needed convincing that it was a waste of time. In the absence of a *bona fide* business plan, people often cling to habits, meaningless activities that don't - and never will - impact business. Some customers, by virtue of their volume and purchasing power, are more valuable than others. Allocating the *right* resources to the *right* customers, with the *right* value proposition, and at the *right* time(s) is what optimally impacts sales. And this is exactly the perspective of the sales *owner*. The sales *owner* sets his or her own goals, makes strategic plans, and works on execution excellence.

On my most productive day, I made only 2 sales calls. To be fair, it was actually a series of calls with two very influential customers. And I was not the only stake *owner* involved. I collaborated with my internal sales partners and the national contracts manager to get a new diabetes therapy approved on a state Medicaid preferred drug list. It was not an easy task, and the state had already denied access to the product once before to patients under its care. But we were confident that our product would help improve the lives of many suffering patients and their families. The challenge was to present the business case to the influencers on the state's medical board and communicate the impact of the value proposition in terms of lives, financial feasibility, and ease of implementation. It required a laser-like focus to deliver a series of presentations over an eight-week period to the two healthcare providers that could make the difference on the decision committee. They were our must-win customers. We focused on making a bold and significant call impact, rather than making an insignificant quantity of calls. In a perfect world, you strive for both quality and quantity. In a less-than-perfect world, productivity always trumps activity. As sales *owners*, we took a calculated risk over the eight weeks to focus on the execution of two very specific calls, often at the expense of not meeting daily reach and frequency metrics. In the end our team was successful. The outcome: product access to over 500,000 managed care lives.

## A LITTLE IRONY

I ran into the same rep who was concerned with his call average. This time, he asked me first *"So, how's your day going?"*

*"Not bad!"* I said, *"We just got a major contract win."*

He followed up with the only question that his *employee* logic could muster, *"So how many calls did you make today?"*

*"Two,"* I replied, *"but they were the right two."*

## TAKE THE NEXT STEP

All businesses boil down to the same two fundamentals: To acquire and retain customers. If you're thinking, *"but my business is different,"* you may be keeping yourself from making progress. However, if you believe that there is more opportunity out there for you or your business, you are probably right.

*Shed old limiting beliefs and think like an owner – it will lead you to where you want to go.*

## About Bob

After earning a degree in mathematics, Bob Sbraccia started his professional career in Actuarial Science. He soon became known for his business acumen and the ability to differentiate by effectively communicating compelling value propositions to business owners, C-level officers, and a wide variety of audiences. His interest turned to business development roles and account management responsibilities, where Bob leveraged his industry knowledge and skills set to attract, acquire, and retain customers. Experienced in both direct and distribution sales models at the local, regional, and national levels, Bob earned national top sales honors 3 times in the Beverage Industry and the Medical Device Industry. A creative problem solver and impactful communicator, Bob also excels at sales training, business coaching, and human performance improvement technologies that are geared toward shortening sales cycles and improving closing ratios.

Mr. Sbraccia is the co-founder of Blue Marble Water Solutions, a Delaware Limited Liability Company, helping Philadelphia area businesses to lock in sustainable cost containment, increase staff productivity, provide better risk management, and give their Green initiative a boost. Got Water?

Bob is also the founder of TrendLine Catalyst, and business consultant for offering outsourced sales solutions and training workshops to help businesses grow bigger and faster.

Visit Bob online at: www.BlueMarbleWater.com
Bob.Sbraccia@BlueMarbleWater.com

# CHAPTER 3

# Six Pillars of Strong Customer Relationships

## By Tracy Myers, CMD

When you want something to last a long time, you need to build it on a strong base. Uncle Frank always said that's why the trees in his yard had to put down firm roots before they started to grow. When we built a new showroom for our car dealership, we dug deep foundations so that it would last for many years and allow us to continue growing.

The same principles apply to one of the most important elements in the success of your business – your customer relationships. You want them to be enduring and continually growing. So they must be built on strong foundations – not simply one-off contacts or slick marketing campaigns.

Over the years, I've discovered that there are <u>six</u> vital pillars that support strong customer relationships. When you put these in place, you will be well placed to have long-lasting, growing relationships with your customers.

The six pillars are as follows.

1. Making the Right First Impression
2. Being Easy to Do Business With
3. Remembering Your Customer Has a Choice

4. Making Life Better for Your Customers

5. Exceeding Expectations

6. Treating Your Customers as Individuals

Each of these pillars has an important role to play and the stronger each of them is, the better your overall relationships will be.

## 1. MAKING THE RIGHT FIRST IMPRESSION

Strong relationships begin with the right first impression. This will determine what people expect from you in future and may even determine whether they stay and do business with you. That first impression can come in many different ways and we have to work on succeeding with each of these elements.

Often these days, the first step is visiting your web site. So have you done what's necessary to make that experience as positive as possible?

Is your web address (URL) simple and easy to remember?

Do your web pages load quickly?

Is the site focused on the customer?

Does it have a look and style that is in tune with your customer base?

Is it easy to read and navigate?

What about when someone calls your store or office on the telephone?

Do people answering the phone have a standard greeting that is friendly and upbeat?

Is the person answering the phone helpful and pleasant to speak with?

Can potential customers speak to someone who is able to answer their questions?

When you have to call someone back, is it always done promptly?

You may believe that all of these elements are working well but you don't know what is happening when you are not around. That's why it's a good idea to check it out. You can either do this yourself or have someone else do it for you as a "mystery shopper." Many business owners have been shocked to find what it's like to be one of their prospective customers.

If you have a brick and mortar shop or office, it also plays a key role in the first impression and the relationship that is established.

What's the first thing customers notice when they walk through your door?

What is the building or neighborhood like?

When people come in, are they greeted by someone or given clear directions?

Is everything clean and fresh so that people enjoy the experience of being there?

If you have a parking lot, is it clean, convenient and well-organized?

Is it easy for customers to approach and talk to your staff?

The sad truth is that too many businesses are making the wrong first impressions on potential customers. This puts many people off becoming customers and means others won't stay long.

If people don't see visiting your store as a positive experience, they will not be coming back and will not be passing the message you want on to others.

However, if you create a strong, positive impression right from the start, people will keep returning and you will have a firm basis for long-lasting customer relationships.

## 2. BEING EASY TO DO BUSINESS WITH

If you want to build strong customer relationships, you have to make sure that it's as easy as possible for people to deal with you. You are in business to take care of your customers and there are some fundamental issues you have to get right as part of that process. It sounds simple but the key to happy customers is often as basic as returning calls, answering e-mails, and addressing complaints promptly.

My support team knows I expect all customer inquiries and problems to be addressed within twenty-four hours if at all possible. They are proud to measure up to that standard.

While we all need to make the best possible use of technology, we need to avoid hiding behind it. When you put the focus on people over technology, you will strengthen the bonds between you, your employees and your customers. If people feel they have some sort of personal contact available, the trust and relationship will be stronger.

If you want to make things easy for your customers, you need to avoid setting up rules and procedures that are designed to make life easy for you rather than for them. It can be too easy to create blocks and obstacles for customers who would otherwise be ready to give you money. Of course, you need to be sensible as a business owner, but you should design your business as much as possible to make things easy for the people who want to give you money.

If you make it easy for people to do business with you, and if you are polite and courteous, you will have happy customers.

## 3. REMEMBERING YOUR CUSTOMER HAS A CHOICE

One thing we can never afford to do is take our customers for granted. We should always remember they can usually go somewhere else to have their needs satisfied. For example, the insurance company that has covered my home for many years has been lobbying me to move my business insurance to them. But I recently had an experience that makes it unlikely I'll be giving them more business.

We suffered some particularly bad weather damage to the house and needed an urgent repair. It was fairly small in terms of cost but the company was imposing strict rules about the way it should be fixed and who should do the work. It was going to take some time to get it all resolved. In the end, it was easier just to get a handyman to do the repair and forget the insurance.

Although I'd been paying them premiums for years – and never claimed a dime – I felt they let me down at the one moment when I was looking to them for assistance. That experience makes it unlikely I'll be giving them more business. They allowed their procedures to get in the way of our relationship and my needs as a customer. Their procedures – which may well be sensible in many situations – made life difficult for me when I needed assistance and they have lost business as a result.

The lesson from that experience is that we often create policies in the heat of the moment that may be an overreaction to something that rarely happens. We then end up creating impediments to the very customers we are trying to help.

If you want to build long-term relationships with your customers, make sure you get rid of any unnecessary policies and procedures that make it harder for them to do business with you. The way to make things easy for your customers is to be able to trust your frontline staff to do what's necessary to serve and please them. That means your frontline staff needs to know that you stand behind them and will not come down on them for trying to please a customer.

The key to building strong relationships with your customers is remembering that your customers have many other places they can go to get what they need. If you remember they have a choice, you will make it easy and enjoyable for them to do business with you!

## 4. MAKING LIFE BETTER FOR YOUR CUSTOMERS

As well as making it easy for your customers to do business with you, you need to remember that the role of your business is to make your customer's life better or easier in some way. They are not doing business with you because they like you or want to help you. They are buying the solutions you offer. That means you have to help them to eliminate their pain points or to make their life better. Your products or services must therefore help to improve their lives or relieve their pain in some way.

At my car dealership, I know there are at least three recurring pain points that customers have regarding buying a nicer, newer car: down payment, monthly payment and financing/credit. That's why I focus on these issues in my advertising and marketing. I have thousands of happy customers so I know that when you cure your customers' pains, you are well on your way to having deep customer relationships. And that's the key to having a profitable business.

If you keep your eyes and ears open on this, you'll be ready to respond immediately when issues arise. Recently I found out that a brand-new customer was having problems with a vehicle he had just bought from us.

I immediately followed up with him and had my support team schedule a VIP Reservation with our service department. In the end, we found out there was not a problem – he had simply gotten some trash in his gas. But the fact that we responded swiftly to his situation not only made him very happy, it also helped to pave the way for a longer relationship, because we had built extra trust.

If you want to keep customers long-term, you have to make their lives easier by alleviating their pain. Prompt follow-up and problem resolution is particularly important for businesses that have a lot of online activity. When customers can feel confident that there are real people looking out for their interests, this helps build trust and loyalty.

When you address pain points with existing customers as soon as they arise – or even before they do – they'll continue to do business with you. To help you deal with these issues before they get out of control, you always need to be listening out for recurring problems. So you need good two-way communication with your customers and with your own staff. When you discover any indications that you're not easy to do business with in some way, make sure you take action to fix it quickly. That's vital to building long-term relationships.

## 5. EXCEEDING EXPECTATIONS

One of the best ways to build deeper relationships with customers is to give them more than they expect. The key to doing that is managing expectations by under-promising and over-delivering. As a customer, you've probably experienced this in both ways – expectations being exceeded or dashed.

You've probably seen it happen in restaurants. You're told the wait will be 30 minutes, and you're seated in 15 minutes. You're very pleased. Your expectations have been managed. But when it works the other way – when you are told 15 minutes and have to wait half an hour – you are not going back there again.

In my dealership, when customers want to finance a vehicle and put $1500 down, I tell them that we can often get customers approved with as little as $1000 down.

But plenty of people drive home after putting no money down. When that happens, I've beaten what I've told them to expect and created a raving fan of my dealership who will immediately go out and tell all their friends.

Managing expectations is crucial to being able to exceed them. This can even work when there are problems. You just need to manage the customer expectations and deliver something better than you promised. Fortunately, poor customer service seems to be so common these days that it can be easy to make customers happy in this way.

## 6. TREATING YOUR CUSTOMERS AS INDIVIDUALS

In a business of any size, it's often easy to think of our customers as a large anonymous group – rather like the crowd at a sports stadium. However, you'll build much better relationships when you learn to envision your target customers as individuals and address your messages more personally to them.

For me, my perfect customer is "Bill." Bill is a twenty eight-year-old husband and father of two with another on the way. Like many other people in today's economic environment, Bill has an 11-year old vehicle with more than 200,000 miles on the clock and it's on its last legs. Bill's pain is that he lost his job a few years back, has had some credit issues and doesn't have any money for a down payment.

I address his pain by offering to help him own the vehicle of his dreams with little or no money down… even with less than perfect credit. Problem solved; pain alleviated; happy customer!

When you have a clear picture of your perfect customer, you can serve them better. For example, I realized that the operating hours of our service department were not ideal for many of our customers. While these hours were typical in my market – closed in evenings and on weekends – I was getting feedback about our accessibility, especially on Saturday and Sunday.

So I began to keep the store open until 7:00 p.m. and opening it on weekends. This was not a popular move with my staff or my competitors. But the results were amazing!

So another aspect of treating customers as individuals is to listen carefully to the feedback they give you. Anything your customer says makes it difficult to do business with you is a pain point for them. You should never view that sort of feedback as a complaint. They are signaling they want to continue doing business with you but are hitting some roadblocks. You should welcome this feedback, as it is often easier for customers to simply walk away. So take notice and get the issue fixed as promptly as possible.

Here's a reminder of the six pillars of building strong customer relationships:

- *Making the Right First Impression: Find out what customers experience when they try to do business with you, especially for the first time.*

- *Being Easy to Do Business With: Make it easy for people to become your customers and build a deeper relationship.*

- *Remembering Your Customer Has a Choice: Get rid of any policies that stand in the way of encouraging customers to do more business with you.*

- *Making Life Better for Your Customers: Always look for new ways to discover and address your customers' pain points.*

- *Exceeding Expectations: Create happy customers by under-promising and over-delivering.*

- *Treating Your Customers as Individuals: Think of your customers as people rather than as a large anonymous mass.*

- *When you put these six pillars firmly in place, you have a strong basis for building healthy long-term relationships and a successful business.*

## About Tracy

Tracy Myers is commonly referred to as The Nations Premier Automotive Solutions Provider. Best-Selling author and legendary speaker Brian Tracy called him "a visionary...a Walt Disney for a new generation."

He is also a Certified Master Dealer and was the youngest-ever recipient of the National Quality Dealer of the Year award by the NIADA, which is the highest obtainable honor in the used car industry. His car dealership, Frank Myers Auto Maxx, was recently recognized as the number one Small Businesses in NC by *Business Leader Magazine*, one of the Top 3 dealerships to work for in the country by *The Dealer Business Journal* and one of the Top 22 Independent Automotive Retailers in the United States by *Auto Dealer Monthly Magazine.*

Myers has been a guest business correspondent on FOX News, appeared on NBC, ABC and CBS affiliates across the country, been featured in USA Today and written for Fast Company. His inspirational stories and strategies for success are in demand across the country – which has given him the opportunity to share the stage with the likes of with Zig Ziglar, James Malinchak, Brian Tracy, Mike Koenig, Bob Burg and Tom Hopkins...just to name a few. His best-selling books help people become better consumers as well as inspire industry leaders to become "game changers." He was also the star of the Telly Award winning film "Car Men."

As the founder of his own marketing and branding academy, Tracy teaches ambitious business owners, professionals and entrepreneurs how to get noticed, gain instant credibility, make millions and dominate their competition.

For more information about Tracy Myers, please visit:
http://www.TracyMyers.com

# CHAPTER 4

# The Difference Between Marketing And Sales: Clinching The Deal

## By Darlene Campbell

Marketing and sales are two very different animals. I learned just what that difference was all about very early in my career - as a matter of fact, it was in my first real job. The lessons I learned there I carried with me throughout my professional life – and helped me immensely in my entrepreneurial efforts, which resulted in creating successful businesses of my own.

Both marketing and sales are, of course, important in their own way. Marketing entails creating the best possible messages about your products and services, then finding the best possible avenues to advertise those products and services with those messages. Sales, on the other hand, is about delivering that message one-on-one to its final destination – your potential customers. When you make the right personal connection, you have the best opportunity to convert a lead to a customer.

### ALL WORK - AND *SOME* PLAY - AT MATTEL

That first real job I spoke of was at Mattel, the world's largest toy company. The company was in the midst of changing their business model when I came on board in my position as Retail Merchandiser. This new direction was instigated by Ruth Handler, who actually started the company while her husband, Elliot, was in the army. When he returned, however, he took over as CEO while she raised their children. To place Mattel's product into stores, the company at that time used mostly men who acted as independent sales reps and placed merchandise that was a good fit in hardware stores (where toys were sold seasonally).

When Ruth came back into the picture, however, she wanted to find new and innovative ways to increase holiday sales orders. She created a new marketing program, which was designed to educate the buyer about the forthcoming line by showing short video clips of TV commercials that would be running nationally from late October through Christmas. Print ads were also produced for the local toy or hardware store to place in local newspapers; a store would typically get a credit towards that local advertising depending on how large an order they had placed.

Ruth thought it important that they augment the mostly-male sales reps with women who would work in the field. She hired five women from across the country for that purpose - and I was very fortunate to be one of them. As I said, I was hired in the role of Retail Merchandiser - there was no indication that anything we did was sales-related. Our job description indicated we were to educate buyers in department stores and smaller toy stores about the total Mattel marketing program - but what we really ended up doing was to reach down to customers in a one-on-one fashion.

We did that by hiring other women to do in-store demonstrations of how action toys worked. These women would set up tables in toy departments and do a "show and tell" of our products on most Saturdays during the holiday shopping season, and then again in the spring to build sales for Easter. These hands-on displays were meant to educate moms and dads about the toys - and, of course, boost sales.

Naturally, this meant that we ourselves had to know how each product worked inside and out, as well as understand the benefit each toy could deliver to a child - the marketing message behind the product. We would spend a very long weekend in July in a hotel in White Plains, New York watching the upcoming TV commercials, as well as actually play with the new line of toys that would be available during the upcoming buying season.

We were *not* allowed to share this information, by the way, before we began going out in the field with the line. We had to sign a strict confidentiality agreement that we wouldn't discuss either the commercials or the toys outside the hotel.

We were also told that *if we left the hotel at any time* during this "sneak preview," we would be dismissed from the company. And they weren't kidding. It seemed like virtually every year someone was willing to test the waters and leave the hotel for whatever reason - and when that "renegade" returned, she would discover that her clothes were packed and that she was told to leave immediately. The reason for this CIA-level of security was that White Plains was very close to New York City and Mattel's trade secrets could be sold there for a pretty penny.

Mattel made sure our training was such that we would make nothing but a positive impression out in the field. We were told what clothing we should wear and instructed in how to interact with store staff as well as families who were potential customers. Incidentally, this was very new territory for a company as big as Mattel - bringing company staff in to work directly with stores and customers was a new and revolutionary process. But it showed me how important the personal touch was and just what motivated individuals to buy from a company. Making the annual journey from the corporate marketing program down to the actual retail level was an ongoing unique business lesson that few get to experience.

I also got to carry a small ball-peen hammer in my briefcase. It wasn't to protect myself - it was to protect the company! If, out in the field, I discovered a toy that was broken or not functioning correctly, I was given strict orders to destroy it with the hammer. Mattel had an excellent quality assurance program that made it possible for a defective toy to be returned, no questions asked, at the local store that carried the line or by mailing it to Mattel's home office. In both cases, the defective toy was replaced with a new one. There were some occasionally unbelievable manufacturing snafus back in those days - including a talking doll that accidentally was programmed to say very unprintable things and cases of Barbies who actually had armpit hair - and you can bet those "misfit toys" weren't around very long once they were discovered.

It was also gratifying to see Mattel be a very good corporate citizen. The week before Christmas, we were instructed to choose orphanages or homes for disabled children, and deliver extra unsold stock (generally kept to replace defective toys) to these places before the 25th. I would call in advance and get the names, ages and interests of each child so that everyone would get the kind of toy they might be wishing for. It was nice to be able to play Santa on such a grand scale and it gave me a very good feeling about my employer.

## BUILDING YOUR BRAND

Mattel was an amazing company to work for - a company that understands the importance of finding ways of building systems that effectively brought their marketing messages directly to the customer level. It inspired me to develop my own style creating that kind of "culture of success" in the businesses I've founded.

Back in 2002, I had the opportunity to really put that kind of culture firmly in place when I decided to rebrand the company. Because change is inevitable – and because it also seems to be coming at a faster pace than ever before in our history – I strongly feel we must consistently evaluate where we are and alter our businesses when necessary. The technological component alone can turn on a dime without warning and necessitate the turnaround of a business's approach. That's why I wanted to put in place a strategic plan that could accommodate this kind of change and build a long-term winning company.

To accomplish this rebranding, I strongly felt I should bring in a mentor – someone who was a successful businessperson or a professional business advisor. I recommend this to anyone – because the right person can help you look objectively at where you've been, where you are and where you need to go in order to continue to grow and succeed.

As I said, in 2002, I was ready to make that kind of significant branding change. My company had begun to provide a different variety of services than we had when we started up fourteen years before; our marketing and even our name no longer reflected what we were all about. I really felt, however, an outside consultant would really help me validate my thoughts about the rebranding.

I hired Paul DelFino of Opportunity Inc., located in Jupiter, Florida, to be that consultant. I wanted him to assess the company as a whole and help me determine the direction we needed to go to grow to the next level. We looked closely at the strengths and the weaknesses of my business, as well as the opportunities and threats to it in the marketplace - not just for the moment, but also three to five years down the road. It was a great experience and really helped me clarify our long-term vision.

Whether you're in the midst of starting up your own operation, or in the middle of this kind of significant rebranding effort, these are the kinds of moments when you have the opportunity to put in place the kinds of systems that Mattel used to great success. Yours undoubtedly will be on a much smaller scale than the toy giant's, but, no matter what your size, the principles remain the same. Carry through your marketing to your actual sales efforts and success can be yours.

## RULES FOR REBRANDING

Here are a few of the big lessons I've learned over the years, both from my experience at Mattel and with my own businesses.

First of all, it's essential in today's world to build a bond of trust with the buyer of your products and/or services. We are experiencing an unparalleled international crisis of confidence in our institutions, simply because we are constantly bombarded with news headlines that showcase new scandals, deceptions and shady business practices.

That means **you need to demonstrate your own credibility in a solid and believable manner.** The best way to do that, in my opinion, is to show your potential customers proof that previous customers have been completely satisfied with your offerings. At my company, Information Communications Group, we do this by spotlighting written testimonials from our current and past clients both on our website and in our printed marketing materials.

Next, **properly train your staff.** Remember how I described Mattel's efforts in making sure we understood their products and how to best present them? Carry that kind of care across to your people. Sales training on any new products or services is a critical key to success. Also determine the role that each team member will play under the new rules and make sure they are as engaged as you are in the new operation. Make sure the tasks are a good fit for each one's personality and skill set.

When you know you have the right buy-in of your philosophy from your staff, focus on training that enhances their skills and mindset. This will not only be a win for your organization, but also a win for them in their professional careers. I believe in ongoing training for my staff, so I purchase business books I think are relevant for my staff to read and report on. Technology has made this process so easy; you just have to download a book and pass it on.

If your rebranding reaches all the way to changing the actual name of your company, I suggest that you **advise the existing customer base of the forthcoming new name** and why the change is being made. People don't like surprises and they might take their business elsewhere if the change confuses them or makes them think they won't be properly served any longer. It's important to reassure them.

A great time to make that kind of big announcement is when you're making customer service calls, mailings or other regular contacts. It doesn't have to be a huge proclamation - just something simple, like..."and by the way, we are changing our name to "X and Y Inc.," because we are now providing products/ services that are different than when we started this company. Nothing really is going to change as far as your purchases are concerned."

Another great tool to use going forward is **the NPS (Net Producer Score) system**. I utilize the NPS once a year and it's really paid off in terms of helping customer retention stay strong and keeping our customer service systems on track. The NPS encourages customer loyalty and measures how many of them are giving your company positive word-of-mouth. We should always reach out to our clients on a regular basis, whether it's by phone, email, "snail mail" or in person, to make sure we are meeting their business needs. These needs change and, again, our business must meet and even anticipate those evolving needs in order to stay successful.

Another way to help customers have a positive attitude about your company is to **let them know about any charitable efforts you have in place**. For example, we have a corporate citizenship program that assists a nonprofit organization that aids thousands of people who need help in our community. I do this because I think it's important to give back, but I also believe it gives our customers the same good feeling about us as I had about Mattel's toy donations.

You should select the nonprofit that is the best fit for your team, your operation and community needs. I have a business friend who started a unique project a few years ago that has grown exponentially - she was even featured on ABC's "Good Morning America" in November 2011 for her efforts. She and her one sales representative (yes I said *"one"*) started collecting new socks for the homeless shelters in the greater Kansas City area. She even asked her clients to participate. The happy result? This year, she collected 4,000 pairs of new socks.

**I also believe all of us business owners need to remember that Customer Service isn't a department;** *IT'S A TOP-TO-BOTTOM EF-FORT.* If you don't have the specific solution a client is looking for, send them to a business that does. Solve problems, don't just relentlessly sell with no regard to actual needs. You make friends (and customers!) for life with that kind attitude - and they'll be the first to recommend you to others.

Finally, never forget how important the "WOW" factor is in your sales efforts. When you actually cause a customer to say, "Wow! I have to tell my friends about this company!" you create your own ever-growing sales forces of fans.

*And with a force like that, singing your praises just because you impressed them, you simply can't lose!*

## About Darlene

Darlene Campbell is known for constantly asking two questions of prospective clients, clients and her peers. "Just what is it that you wish to accomplish?" And, "It is all about your return on investment, isn't it?" Whether the questions she asks applies to their organization or government assessments on their business and income, she feels strongly that if they can get the answers right in the beginning the task becomes simpler to accomplish.

Darlene explains that there is a way to outsource many of the processes to the solution to be effective, efficient and give a return on the investment. She founded what has come to be known as Information Communications Group in 1986, a multi-lingual company that supplies inbound and outbound call center services for messaging, telemarketing, order taking, surveys, appointment setting, server monitoring and email management – a company that designs call center processes to get results!

To learn more about Darlene Campbell and Information Communications Group visit: www.infocg.com or call Toll free: 1-800-547-2213.

www.informationcommunicationsgroup.com

# CHAPTER 5

# How to Survive and Thrive in a Down Economy... or any Economy

## By Kathy Hagenbuch

I think we can all agree...it is glaringly obvious that the business landscape has forever changed – drastically. Whether you blame it all on the tanking of our economy, or you believe in the past predictions that our society would inevitably evolve into more of a consumer-driven economy, no matter your industry, the size of your business, whether you operate offline or online, the fact remains that in order to 'maximize your business exposure, dominate your market and explode your profits,' you need to make adjustments to fit the new way consumers do business – or perish.

Statistics show that where consumers hang out, where they spend their time, how they communicate, how and where they search for goods and services, and how they make buying decisions is radically different than even a mere few years ago.

So whether you are in sales, an online marketer or an offline bricks and mortar, local mom and pop establishment – and I've been all three – the 'billion dollar' question remains...do you become as obsolete as the manual typewriter and the horse and buggy, or do you make the necessary adjustments to keep your business alive, thriving and profitable? Are you in it to win it?!

Most entrepreneurs go into business because they love what they are doing and they are really good at it. However, the business and marketing side of things is usually a weak spot that suffers and can drive them right out of business. That combined with the reality of the hectic and fast-paced business environment, leaves little time for the small business owner to learn how to run their business or research and understand the marketing strategies that will help their company grow.

The result is that traditionally, small business owners have no plan to bring in more clients, keep the clients they have and to get more referrals. Even though I knew I needed to do something to get more clients in the door, I remember being so busy trying to run my business, that like most small business owners, I threw money at whatever showed up in my email inbox or at whoever came through my front door.

Since I didn't have the time to do the research on the best ways to market and build my business, I assumed – and hoped – that the salespeople coming into my business must know what would help make my business make more money. So I threw money at their strategies without having any idea what my business really needed, or whether or not their strategies would bring what I most needed in my business – and I hoped for results.

I, like many other small business owners, learned the hard way that that is a very inefficient and costly way to do business. Both from the perspective of time, money and resources to implement the wrong strategies and the cost of lost revenue by not implementing the right ones.

Here's an example that you may even relate to. Not long ago, a very smart gentleman came to me in despair telling me that if he wasn't able to turn his business around within two months, he was going to have to shut it down. When I took a look at his business, I could quickly see that there was a major disconnect in what he was selling and what people actually found when they came to his website.

He spent a lot of time and money making connections and driving people to his website to sell his software classes, but when his prospects came to his site, they found something completely different. And the 'giveaway' he used on his site had nothing to do with the problems his target market had and the reason they came to his site in the first place. So unfortunately, the traffic he worked so hard to get to his site left in confusion without ever having the opportunity to solve their problems and see how brilliant this gentleman was at delivering the solution they so desperately needed.

The same is true in marketing for your business. If the marketing strategy you implement isn't the right one for where you are in your business right now, the results will be dismal and your money will be wasted.

Recognizing that often the solution is simple and right in front of you, I incorporated the simple and effective tools and leverage strategies I've used to identify the hidden profit centers in my own business, as well as those I have used in the 25 plus years that I have been helping small business owners boost their business profits, into the Profit Acceleration System™.

Designed to work with the way the entrepreneurial brain is 'naturally wired' rather than forcing you to fit the traditional mold and 'cookie cutter' business models, it will allow you to get an immediate picture of where your business is right now, and what is necessary to plug the holes where you are leaving money on the table, and increase your profits.

So let's start with the basic seven-step framework of the Profit Acceleration System™ to help you determine what you can do to thrive in any economy:

1. **Identify what you want in your business**: I realize this isn't the sexiest and most fun thing to do, but if you don't know what you want in your business, it's impossible to know what you need to do to fix problems, reduce costs and increase profitability.

   The Profit Acceleration System™ includes tools that help you easily identify exactly what you want in your business, specifically what you need to do each day to achieve that, and which ideas and strategies you should implement now to give you the 'biggest bang for your buck.'

2. **Identify what you most need in your business right now**: Once you know what you want in your business, you must identify what you most need or what's currently missing – that if it were present, would make the most significant difference in your business and profitability.

   At different times, your business needs different things to keep profits up and expenses down. And quite often your business may be weak in more than one area and the areas can also be interconnected. When you identify exactly what your business needs *most right now*, you can match the marketing strategy and campaigns that are most likely to get you that result.

   Following are six areas to look at to help you determine where you need to focus your energy, efforts and resources.

   • **Rev up your marketing engine** – 90% of consumers use the internet to find and research products or services in their local area. Who will your target audience find when they are looking for the products and services you provide - you or your competition?

      82% of people performing an online local search follow-up via an online inquiry, phone call or visit to an offline local business. Searchers decide which local business to spend their money with – by who and what they find on the Internet.

      Most often your online presence and website will be your prospects first experience of you and your business. If your potential clients find you, will what they see to make your prospects eager to do business with you – or make them skip your business and go on to your competition?

      92% of all local searches carried out will eventually convert to a sale. Optimizing your local presence will make you visible to the 86% of Americans who search on a mobile phone.

      Do you have a website that is worthy of the products and services you provide and will make your clients stop their search and buy from you? Is your local presence optimized so that you show up in a mobile search? If not, now is definitely the time to rev up your marketing engine.

- **Get clients / generate leads** – If you feel your business needs exposure to prospects who have never had any experience of you and your products or service, then generating leads and getting clients may be where you need to focus your efforts and resources right now.

  While you should always have a steady stream of leads flowing into your pipeline, don't forget about strategies that capitalize on the hidden gold in your existing database. Since it costs 85% more to get a new customer than it does to get an existing customer to spend more money with you, make sure you are considering strategies that do both.

- **Convert Leads to Clients** – It's no secret that people do business with those they know, like, and trust. If your business is swimming in leads but you've not been able to capitalize on the revenue resulting from converting those leads to clients, then this is an area you need to focus on.

- **Service Your Clients** – Now that you have converted leads to clients, it is essential that you provide the same exceptional VIP service or quality product to each and every client, no matter who in your business delivers the product or service.

  Two-thirds of customers do not feel valued by those servicing them, and according to US News and World Report, we lose 82% of clients because of poor service and staff indifference. How does your company measure up to those statistics? If there is room for improvement, this might be an area you should focus on.

- **Client Retention and Referrals** – The average company loses 10% of its customers each year. If your business can boost profits from 25% to 125% simply by retaining 5% of it's existing clients, it stands to reason that you must have a strong client retention program in your business.

  And since happy customers tell 4 to 5 others of their positive experience, a referral program should be an integral part of your overall marketing mix.

  If you have a lot of clients who aren't repeatedly buying from you or are buying only once, this is an area you may need to look more closely at.

- **Follow up system** – The sale is just the beginning. 68% of business revenue in America is lost due to lack of follow up after the sale. That is a lot of money and profits walking right out your front door.

  This is totally preventable by simply adding a good follow up system to show your clients they mean more to you than just the 'cha-ching' of the cash register. There are many fun, creative and effective ways to follow up with your clients, including a combination of email, video email, cards, postcards, texting, mobile apps, social media, an online community on Facebook or a private members area.

### 3. Identify the marketing strategy or strategies that will help you accomplish the result you currently want or need in your business:

Now that you know exactly where your business might be losing clients and revenue and what your business most needs to plug those leaks and boost profits, it is essential to eliminate the archaic and antiquated business models and marketing methods that may have worked in the past. Exchange them for fresh, cutting-edge and proven profit strategies that get you maximum exposure where your prospects and clients are hanging out.

For example, it doesn't make sense to advertise in the Yellow Pages telephone book when your prospects are searching on their mobile phones and on the Internet for the type of product or service you provide.

If you are contemplating any of what I call the 'big three' or 'Lo, Mo & So' (Local, mobile marketing and social media), you are on the right track for sure.

Maximize your results by leveraging your marketing strategies so you can double and triple dip simply by the way they are implemented and the campaigns designed around them.

A well-planned and well-thought out mobile marketing campaign can help you get new clients, make it easier for your clients to do business with you, provide a good follow up system, help you get referrals and make you stand out from your competition. Therefore, your clients *stay with you*—preventing you from losing 10% of your clients each year.

4. **Implement**: Putting your strategies to work for you as quickly as possible is essential to increasing your profits.

   Outsourcing and using existing staff members in the implementation of your marketing strategies allows you to spend your time running your business – rather than taking time away from your clients to learn the ins and outs of the latest marketing strategy.

   Remember, the quicker to the marketplace, the quicker you see results.

5. **Test, Track and Measure**: The secret to doubling the effectiveness of your marketing is measurement. Test, track and measure everything you do so you can determine what's working and should be repeated, what's not working that with a little adjustment might work better, and what you just need to dump all together. The Profit Acceleration Money Game™ will easily help you do just that.

   Make sure you know what you are trying to measure when you implement a new marketing strategy, and be diligent in keeping up with the measurement process as your campaign unfolds.

6. **Identify your crash points:** Your crash points are areas in your business systems, marketing strategies, etc., where things fall apart resulting in frustration, lost revenue, unhappy clients and dissatisfied staff. Oftentimes, pinpointing where things fall apart will illuminate a simple and easy fix – to get things back on track.

7. **Repeat:** Go back to step one and repeat the process weekly or at least monthly to identify what is working and what is not. Repeat what works, adjust where you can and dump what doesn't work.

   Overlooking this step results in too much time passing without knowing if what you are doing is working, or if the needs of your business have changed. Every moment you continue to do something that isn't working or doesn't fit the current and immediate needs of your business, is revenue and profits lost!

As you work through the Profit Acceleration System™ it's important to remember a couple of things.

*First*, remember that as you are adding some of the desperately needed components to your business that don't put immediate cash into your pocket, you need to keep a good balance of money-making strategies in place as well.

*Second*, a university studied successful sales people who were making over $250,000 a year – looking for the commonality. The one thing they all had in common that helped them to make that kind of money was: Speed of Implementation – or the length of time between when you hear about or learn something, and when you put it into action. Highly successful people got an idea and put it into action immediately rather than sitting around thinking about it.

Whether the speed of implementation applies to the Profit Acceleration System™ steps or in the implementation of the ideas you are getting in this chapter or this book, the key is to get moving!

Sometimes it can be a bit tricky to identify exactly what your business needs to pull it out of stagnancy and boost profits. However, armed with the statistics in this chapter, this allows you to see how your business measures up. With the Profit Acceleration System™ formula, you can zero in on exactly where you can leverage your efforts, your resources and your results and *thrive* – not just survive – *in our NEW ECONOMY*.

## About Kathy

Kathy Hagenbuch is a best selling author and local online, social media and mobile marketing expert with a proven track record of helping her clients obtain results and put more money in their pockets. She is the founder of Extreme Results Now! and the Profit Acceleration Implementation Team, a company that eliminates the stress, time and exorbitant cost of learning and implementing new marketing strategies by providing effective, turn key 'done for you' marketing services for clients nationwide.

Seen in *USA Today*, Yahoo! Finance, CBS Money Watch and many others, Kathy reminds her small business clients that in today's consumer-driven economy, it is essential for a business whose very survival depends upon revenue from local clientele, to eliminate the archaic and antiquated marketing methods and traditional cookie cutter business models considered the 'industry norm,' but produce mediocre results – at best.

Kathy's Profit Acceleration System™ is geared for the reality of the hectic and fast-paced business environment and will help you to identify hidden profit centers in your business, maximize your exposure, dominate the presence in your market, and get found where your prospective clients are looking. This system achieves results by implementing fresh, cutting-edge and proven leverage and profit strategies, resulting in more clients, reduced costs, less stress, and higher profits.

To increase your profits, get 'Extreme Results' with Kathy's unique small business and entrepreneur tools - AND grab your Free Special Report 'Your Profit Explosion Guide: Capitalize on the Hidden Profits in Your Business,' visit:
www.BoostBusinessProfits.com/inittowinit
or
www.IncreaseSalonProfits.com/inittowinit.

CHAPTER 6

# TIPS FOR CONSUMERS HOW TO EVALUATE YOUR SALES-PERSON

By Pinny Ziegler

### AN ALL TOO COMMON STORY

John and Susan both have had what you could unfortunately call a normal experience in the consumer world.

John grew up assuming every salesperson had proper training and represented the paragon of his or her industry. Susan assumed that whatever she ordered came as advertised and at the best price.

Over time, both became inured and hardened to salespeople, whether it was the time John was sold on crucial office supplies but the distributor was constantly out of stock and always late on delivery, or the time Susan ordered fabric samples for her online retail business only to get the wrong color in the mail.

In the first situation, John jumped at the opportunity to get a copy machine by an unproven brand at a fraction of the cost, only to see it break down a week later.

Call after call, no one ever came out to fix the machine and this was the same company from which he was ordering other key products like paper. John was locked into an unhealthy relationship.

In Susan's case, she not only got the wrong color in the mail but after the mix up, the salesman didn't care to make things right and even had the nerve to try and sell her on additional products. He didn't care to ask how to correct the first mistake.

Now here's the shocker - **John and Susan are actually you!**

We have all built up an impenetrable wall because of the negative experiences in business relations. We have this communication paralysis that forces us to close off to all salespeople because of a stigma or a story we may have overheard. But, just like John and Susan, we often need the product that these people have to sell us.

It is the ultimate "Catch-22."

The bottom line is that having a trusted ally in the form of a salesperson is the greatest asset a business can have. If you know how to handle, talk with and build relationships with salespeople, you can decide if what they have to offer is right for you and your business.

I, like you, have dealt with salespeople that are not helpful, not knowledgeable or just don't care. And if they do care, they often keep calling and pressing the business, not focusing on the needs of what's important to me as the customer.

I can't put it in any other way but that this was my motivation to go out and try to learn the right approach in selling. I wanted to learn how to give the consumer a buying experience that they would look forward to and thus my journey started.

My insatiable hunger for knowledge led to reading all and anything I could get my hands on.

My first book I read on sales was *How to Master the Art of Selling Anything* by Tom Hopkins. I followed that up with hours of books and blogs from the top teachers in the field of selling. From then on, I was consumed with the task of finding the right people to coach me on "proper" selling. I was privileged enough to land with two of the most prominent mentors in the craft.

Now here is the most basic foundation of selling - **The customer loves buying but he doesn't love being sold – Plain and simple!** The great salesman has the knowledge or talent of how to make the consumer feel like he is buying instead of pushing them to purchase their product and having the consumer feel like they were sold.

The need to apply what I learned to my daily situations caused me to contemplate deeply, which led me to a frightful conclusion - *Untrained salesmen hurt the customers just as much as they hurt themselves.*

## THE 80/20 RULE

The 80/20 Rule or the Pareto Principle is simple. The top 20 percent of the sales force is selling 80 percent of the product. Scary but true. That means that 80 percent of the force is NOT getting its message across to the client – You!

Their product may be great, the need may be justified, but their method of presenting is wrong. I learned from Chet Holmes, author of the book *The Ultimate Sales Machine*, that more than 90 percent of people, when being presented with an offer to buy, are not in the buying mode.

Hence, they actively fail to listen or pay attention to what's being offered. That means the chance for you, the consumer, to be hurt and lose out on an essential product is very great.

An age-old story starts with a customer abruptly turning away a salesman because he thinks he is not interested in the product. A few months later, that same customer is approached with the same product by a different salesperson. This time, the customer bites.

Why?

The presentation is the only thing that changed. Obviously, the customer DID want what was being sold. In that case, the customer could have benefited from the product all this time and has lost out.

And then it dawned on me.

Why not take the vast knowledge that I learned in selling and transform that into a powerful list of rules consumers can use, and give them the power to make their buying experience a pleasurable one? Even with the 80/20 rule everyone can become a Rumpelstiltskin and turn straw into gold.

Do not immediately say "No!" or "Just send me information."

When requesting information, the salesman will just send you generic information that you'll throw into a dark, gloomy cabinet never to be seen again. As Herbert Hoover said, "Wisdom often comes of knowing what to do next."

So, here we go with my four vital, yet easy to understand rules for successful buying.

## FOUR SIMPLE RULES FOR SUCCESSFUL BUYING

These are four key rules for the consumer to help build those illustrious, golden connections. This is why we are in business – to make a connection, a synergy beneficial to both parties.

### Rule #1: Referrals
– Information is power and asking for referral letters from a sales representative supplied by satisfied clients is a crucial step. Read what they have to say and even call them to ask what their experience has been with the company. To get referrals, even out of satisfied clients, is a big achievement. When you are asked to take a survey after a sales experience, good or bad, your first instinct is to say, "No." So getting a referral shows something about the company and salesman. It is something that is valuable.

### Rule #2: Features and Benefits
– Many people mix up the understanding of Benefits and Features. Suppliers pride themselves with all sorts of different features they offer to their client base. Powerful consumers need to be aware of these features and turn them in to something that can be a benefit for their business.

Just a quick example – When a supplier boasts that they have 10,000 items in stock, that doesn't mean much to you at first, especially when you don't sell 10,000 items in your store. But if you think more about it, the order turnaround time is quicker with this surplus and eliminates the need for back orders. Now, you can supply YOUR consumer in a timely fashion without headaches and keep your clients satisfied. Any delays can lose you customers and ruin your reputation.

Another standard example is when businesses offer next day delivery. You hear this offer all the time and it usually doesn't mean anything to you, it's just a feature. The customer and the salesperson don't break it down into dollars and cents. By having a supplier that can ship next day can mean a greater cash flow since you don't have to stock up a lot of inventory. Saving time and relieving stress can also have a money value. It's important to take the features being offered and imagine what can be done with that.

When looking over the materiel presented to you, think, "Can this feature be a money-saving benefit for me?" That's the question.

### Rule #3: Guide Your Salesperson
– Once you're actually interested in what's being offered, it is very important to convey to the salesman exactly what you want in the business relationship. In almost every lost sale there is a reason why it went sour. Many times, the consumer simply didn't connect with the sales representative and this had almost nothing to do with price, a common misconception.

**This leads us to the four basic personality types.**

My goal is not to teach a college course in personalities but give you a glimpse of how we differ in nature. That leads to different needs in communication. Getting a brief description of these personalities will help you open up to what you need as an individual.

Dr. Tony Alessandra in *The Platinum Rule* coined four distinct behaviors that are vital for consumers to understand.

**D-Director**

**S-Socializer**

**R-Relator**

**T-Thinker**

### The Director
A director is more dominant and prone to driving people. They are not shy or modest and action is what excites them. It's often said they make

things happen, they're impatient and they're not about praise. **Their greatest fear is being soft.**

### The Socializer
He lives on being social, likes exciting ventures, good times and a good audience. Socializers love people who are fast-paced, energetic and outgoing, and who are also feeling-based. They seek admiration. **Their greatest fear is not being liked.**

### The Relator
The relator operates at a slow, steady pace. They like tranquility and stability. They are great team players that understand everyone and want to understand your point of view. The Relator is a feelings-based person but in a more subtle way. He will listen more than talk. **Their greatest fear is change.**

### The Thinker
This is an ego person like a director, and does not like too many questions or personal touch. He or she just wants to be logical, pragmatic and is cautious of making a mistake. What excites them is reason and logic. **Their greatest fear is irrationality.**

We don't need a Ph.D. to know that an efficient sale is when there is not just a sale being closed, but a new relationship being built. The ideal situation is when the sales representative understands the needs of the client and his or her personality. Furthermore, if a client knows himself and what's important to him in a sale, he will be able to see if a relationship is a benefit or not. Then, he can guide the sale.

For example, as a <u>Director</u> type of personality, you might convey that meetings are not important. Facts are what matter to a Director; facts on how you can help them make their company more efficient.

As a <u>Socializer</u>, you may want your salesman to visit you once a month. Other people might not want that personal touch, but no matter what, everyone has a preference.

As a <u>Relator</u>, a personal guarantee would be something that would be important and that the sales representative is there to help if the need arises.

However, as a <u>Thinker</u>, you may want all the detail in front of you clearly, so you can make a rational decision.

## Rule #4: Stay Current With Your Sale

– A lot of businesses set a vendor in place and get comfortable. This is a natural relaxation you must fight. A few years can quickly pass until you review what your current vendor supplier is giving you. The situation may have changed and it may not be to your liking, or certain aspects may have changed for the better and you're not taking advantage of them! It's a pity to invest belief and trust in a relationship with a vendor and then have to start all over again. Instead, once a year or more, make sure to schedule time to go over details that may have changed.

The possible outcome with leaving an arrangement as it is and not adjusting it accordingly can be negative for both parties involved. First, a competitor comes in after a while and says, "What! You are paying so much for that?" He slams the prices down and offers a rate 20 percent cheaper. Be wary of this. Sometimes, that great price is just offered to get you locked in or the product may not be comparable. Now you, the customer, were seduced by an inferior product and lost a long-time business relationship.

In the end, you just need to be honest with yourself, as well as the salesperson, in order to get what you want throughout the life of any sales relationship. It may take some time but asking questions and opening yourself up by tearing down that wall will result in the greatest asset of all. Avoid that cheap, instant gratification and learn to evaluate your salesperson to see if this is a bond that can benefit both parties for years to come – rather than just the short life of the purchase.

## PERSONAL NOTE

Since I was a young child, I've had a bad experience when going out to buy anything in the commercial world. This hurt me so much that I was motivated to be the kind of person to go out and sell in such a way as to make the consumer happy.

This is easier said than done.

The consumer, myself included, has built such an impenetrable wall around him that the salesperson doesn't know how to chisel away at it. Sometimes, it is not just the price or the tangible assets a sale has to offer, but it's a simple "Hello" that is going to seal the deal.

## About Pinny

Pinny Ziegler started his sales career in 2002, focusing on honesty and dedication for his clients. The current situation in sales, including from a lack of knowledge by a salesperson to a lack of respect for the consumer, hurt Pinny in such a way that he spent countless hours with the best coaches in the business.

He was consumed with becoming a salesman who could connect with any type of customer and build a pure relationship on a foundation of trust and mutual respect. His customer's happiness is just as important, if not more important, than his.

More than 10 years after he started in sales, Pinny still consults with coaches and stays current on new techniques that can help him make a real connection. He believes the sale doesn't end when money is exchanged but, in fact, it's just the beginning.

His passion to inspire people to reach their goals led him to found a support group Focus To Succeed for small business and salesmen based on the foundations needed to succeed - Focus, Creativity and Accountability.

Pinny lives in his hometown of Brooklyn, New York with his beautiful and loving wife Fagie and their children. His goal is to raise happy, confident and caring individuals to someday enter the workforce and make the same type of meaningful contributions to the community.

*"With honesty and integrity, I will do whatever it takes to get the job done right." – PZ*

# CHAPTER 7

# MANAGING EXPECTATIONS

## By Paul Edgewater

This chapter will cover managing expectations in the business arena. We all want to meet and exceed our clients' expectations, and this should be the goal of every businessperson. In order to meet and exceed clients' expectations, those expectations need to be managed. It is one of the secrets for providing stellar service. Managing expectations needs to be one of your main focuses for whatever product or service you are providing.

Think of your own experiences in business. Whenever you got more than you bargained for, the memory is a sweet one. Whenever the converse is true, the experience can sour a business relationship enough to end it. Unfortunately, it's very easy for this to happen and it's not because anything nefarious has taken place, or that the entity making promises unrealistically set the bar of expectations too high either. The ability to manage expectations comes with experience.

Not managing expectations is at the root of most failings when dealing with people – both in business and in our personal lives. If we've ever been burned in business, it's because our expectations weren't met. If our hearts have ever been broken, it's because our expectations weren't met. Something was supposed to—or not supposed to—happen, or some-one was supposed to do—or not do—something. In either case, the expected result was not what the outcome ended up being. The consequence is always the same – disappointment because expectations weren't met.

What does it take to manage expectations? In a nutshell, it comes down to only taking on what you can effectively execute with the resources at hand. If a business is a new one, very often the proprietor is anxious about securing business and will sometimes agree to terms before resources are secured to properly execute; be it in personnel, equipment or specialized knowledge. But this can also happen to the seasoned business professional that may be hurting for business and will agree to, or say anything to secure the business. These folks may think that everything will fall into place once the wheels start moving, but very often it doesn't. Whether you're new or experienced, don't ever fall into this trap. When I was a child, I often heard a saying in response to some kid talking 'big' on the playground: "Don't let your mouth write a check that your butt can't cash." As an adult, I found that this more than applies to running a successful business.

At my company, the rare times something hasn't gone right in the eyes of our clients is because we as a company didn't properly manage their expectations (I'm very grateful those occasions have been few-and-far-between). In our case, the reasons for this can often be traced back to working with a third party who made promises without consulting us. Sometimes expectations are set in brainstorming sessions, which is a mistake. That's an environment where all ideas are on the table. That's where concepts are born, not where the executional minutia is estab-lished. Problems manifest when those sessions are revisited without an objective review of how viable the expectations are. Of course, every-one would like to meet and exceed all expectations and every company does their best to do this, but it's a good idea to sometimes lower the bar. It's best to 'under promise and over deliver.'

Back in 2004, my company produced a conference for NRC (now called Avid Ratings: AvidBuilder.com) and the keynote, Paul Cardis, CEO of NRC, cited an excellent example of managing expectations (for those who aren't familiar with this company, they are basically the J. D. Power of home builders here in the States). A portion of his talk covered a somewhat common phenomenon in home building; as a new house settles, the foundation will sometimes crack. This is an important customer service and public relations issue for builders. If enough people file complaints to the Better Business Bureau about cracked foundations in new homes, it could potentially sink a homebuilder. How should a homebuilder address this? By managing expectations. Mr. Cardis told his audience that homebuilders shouldn't hide the fact that foundations may crack. Instead, he urged builders to preemptively inform all homebuyers that not only can their foundations crack—but that they WILL crack!

Does that come as a shock to you? It did to me. Even though all foundations won't crack (and most don't), is it a good idea to tell someone who just gave you perhaps hundreds of thousands of dollars (or more) for a new home, that the foundation is going to crack? Apparently yes. The reader is probably quicker than I, but just in case you need some clarification; if you don't disclose everything to someone who just made perhaps the largest investment of their lives, and something like a foundation cracks, you're going to have trouble. If however, you preemptively tell them that it is going to happen, you have properly managed expectations. Put yourself in the position of that homebuyer. If while you are being shown the property, the agent tells you something to the effect: "This is a new home which was built on cleared land. The ground under the home was formally a cornfield and never supported anything heavier than a tractor. After all the tons of concrete, wood, bricks, roofing, windows, flooring, etc. are piled on top of the ground, it's common and expected that the foundation will crack with settling. We, of course, take all measures to prevent this, but most of the time, it will crack. If and when that happens, we of course will come and fix it free of charge for the first five years of ownership after which time, the home will have settled properly so as to prevent this from being a chronic condition."

Now you, as the homebuyer, have been prepared for your foundation to crack. If and when it does, you take it in stride because your expectations have been managed properly. If however, the builder chooses not to disclose this information to you, and should your foundation break, you're calling 60 Minutes or John Stossel, and the builder has a big problem and an even bigger PR issue. Let's say the foundation never cracks (which is the most likely scenario), now this customer is telling everyone within earshot how great their house is and how amazing it is that the foundation didn't crack. That represents new business for the builder while the former scenario represents lost and never-to-be-had business. Use this example and think of the dollar value of managing expectations properly in your business. Whatever your business is, think of your average transaction, and do the math. Not just with one client, but with all the word-of-mouth clients that will either be generated or kept forever at bay.

You may be saying to yourself, "I already do that," and maybe you do. That's great. May I suggest that you go a step further and tell your clients to expect something negative when the odds flesh out that it hardly ever happens? I'm not suggesting that you stretch the truth here. If a potential scenario has never happened before and in all likelihood won't, don't present it as such. But if the potential scenario has been demonstrated to have happened in the past with some degree of consistency, then present is as something to be on the look out for. It's always best to under promise and over deliver. Remember, that negative scenario may end up happening after all. This way, you've covered your bases.

In the promotions industry, we often work with two or more parties when planning events. It's vital to our reputations that we stay on top of the expectations of the party paying the bills. It's a balancing act to be sure; reassuring the client that the outcome they desire is something your company can deliver (so they do in fact do business with you) and not overselling yourself (which ensures a one-time-only transaction, lost revenue and bad blood). We must exercise due diligence with these third parties. If they are promising the world to the client and they then bring us in as the fall guys, who takes the fall? We do. It's vital to be included in on all conceptual and planning meetings. I can't tell you how many times we have been brought into a project that should never have left the brain storming session it was originally brought up in. A perfect example of this was with one of our best clients, who shall remain unnamed. A number of years ago, this client approached us with an ambitious project of decorating a large number of their prominent stores with holiday decorations. We had been working with this client in many areas of the country for years, and already had a solid relationship. As a result, we were recommended to this particular region for the project, which we were initially grateful for, but later lamented. We flew out to meet with them and the project (as it was presented to us) seemed to be only in need of a vendor to execute it (us). Little did we know that internally, the expectations of this company's brass had already been raised to unrealistic levels by well-meaning marketing folks who, to say the least, hadn't taken everything into consideration.

The plan was to cover their stores top to bottom and in and out with holiday lights. The effect was to be grand; the same way a certain someone in your neighborhood goes the extra mile when doing their holiday decorations on their home. It was to be magnificent. It was to be news worthy. It was to be spectacular and we wanted nothing more than to deliver the goods. The challenge though, was that our client hadn't cleared any of this internally before bringing us in. No legal counsel, no operations, no risk management, no facilities—nothing and no one. In hindsight, we weren't really given the job of executing this event as it was planned; we were given the job of reining in the entire scope of the project.

Right away, we discovered that no one had bothered to check to see if the stores had enough electrical service to support all the lights requested. (They didn't. Not one store had the reserve power.) Even if the stores could have all the lights on them without blowing every circuit, the lawyers wouldn't allow any lights to be installed on the stores that could be reached by customers or their kids (either deliberately or accidentally). The end result was that we lined the cornices and roof lines of the stores with strings of lights; something that the property managers at most of these stores did anyway at no extra charge to the tenants as a part of their lease.

Guess who ended up holding the bag? The lawyers? Nope. Risk management? No, guess again. Facilities? Try again. The marketing people? You get one more guess. That's right: our company. We were tarred and feathered and had the door of future business in this region slammed in our face. And why did that happen? Because we didn't manage expectations properly. In essence, we didn't tell them that their foundations were going to crack—and they did—big time. What makes this all the worse is that we did everything we possibly could have done to make this promotion a success—except manage expectations. I can't put an exact dollar figure on this, but based on the volume of business we get from other regions that this client serves, it's many hundreds of thousands of dollars. In business, more often than not, we only get one opportunity at bat.

This was a hard lesson, and was the impetus behind a checklist that we now use whenever expectations and goals are established, or we are brought into a project that has already been planned without our input. It is the best way to ensure that no one is left disappointed, and more importantly, that your client is happy and will reach out to you for future projects. Of course you should customize this list to reflect your services or product offerings, but it's a great start. Whatever you do, just be sure you manage all expectations—your clients and your own.

## EXPECTATION CHECKLIST:

- What are the current expectations?
- Who established them?
- How many parties were/are involved in the planning?
- Who are they?
- Who set the budget? Is it flexible?
- Are current expectations possible to be executed within given parameters?
- Has legal counsel been retained for this project?
- Have risk management and facilities been consulted?
- How much creative time has already been invested?
- What logistical work has already been done?
- Establish roles and responsibilities.
- Rein in expectations and under-promise.
- Over deliver.

## About Paul

Best selling and award winning author Paul Edgewater, is CMO & co-founder of Chicago, IL-based, Busy Bee Promotions, Inc. Busy Bee opened its doors in 1998 and conducts an average of 400 events monthly coast-to-coast.

Paul has been featured in the *Wall Street Journal, USA Today, Promo Magazine*, and on FOX News, CNN, CNBC, MSNBC, FOX, ABC, NBC and CBS news affiliates promoting products and services for clients such as Coca-Cola, Starbucks Coffee, Verizon Wireless, Groupon, Whole Foods Market, Macy's and many, many more. His specialty is in maximizing his clients' exposure in and out of their respective market places by executing very unconventional, attention-getting tactics including an acclaimed, free-20-second spot he garnered for Starbucks Coffee on Fox News by rattling off talking points while doing "360s" on a branded Segway Personal Transporter!

Paul is the author of "The Book On Promotions" series, *"COUNTER ATTACK - Business Strategies For Explosive Growth In The New Economy"* co-authored with world-renowned business leader, Brian Tracy, *"The Only Business Book You'll Ever Need"* co-authored with Robert G. Allen and *"It's All Up To You - The Top 10 Things You Should Know To Have The Best Life Possible"*, co-authored with best-selling author, speaker and coach, Grace Daly (all available at: www.PaulEdgewater.com). He has more than 30 years of sales, marketing and promotions experience and is motivated by his intense love of the private sector and the free market system, and takes great pleasure in creatively connecting his clients with new customers.

In addition to his business pursuits, he is a weekend athlete with three marathons under his belt and also an accomplished musician and animal lover.Paul lives steps off the Magnificent Mile in beautiful downtown Chicago and is available for speaking engagements and consultations.

For booking information or to contact Paul directly, visit:
www.BusyBeePromotions.com.
Or call Toll-Free: 1-888-438-9995.

# CHAPTER 8

# SECRETS TO BUILDING A WORLD-CLASS BUSINESS THROUGH LEADERSHIP MARKETING

## By Vince Ferraro

During this economic recession, companies are focused on increasing earnings and revenue. Many companies that were hit by the economic downturn in 2007 are still struggling to bring sales back up to pre-recession levels. These companies are trying to determine the size of the current market and establish a new baseline for growth. In many cases, these companies are not prepared to grow new markets, because their management team has failed to deliver new business and growth opportunities.

Many companies fail to realize that they must have a diverse portfolio of product lines to be successful. Marketing executives tend to categorize these portfolios of products into core, scale, and new business interests. Core products are the slowly growing or declining, highly profitable, traditional business interests that spin off a lot of cash. An example is Kodak's traditional film business.

Scale products have growth, established market success, and profitability. HP's LaserJet printer is a good example of a scale product. HP could not build enough of them. The key issue regarding scale is how to take a product from ten thousand to one million units a month, while building the organizational capabilities, infrastructure, and processes needed to achieve that level of success.

Finally, new products are those that show future growth but have limited revenue and profitability today. The goals for new products are to expand to capture a broader market share, reduce costs, and stabilize quality. The underlying assumption is new products and businesses will grow (scale) in the future.

There isn't always a clear distinction between the three product categories, as scale products and some new products can be embedded within or operated adjacent to core products. There are many books that discuss product life cycle management and a number of models that can help companies understand the process.

This is where a marketing leader comes into play. In many companies, marketing is relegated to the corporate marketing functions of branding, advertising, PR, communications, social media, and the Web. These are very important functional areas of responsibility for marketing, but because of a lack of measurement on the return on investment, guess what happens when times are tough? Marketing expenses get whacked because, as market leaders, we have failed to deliver hard numbers to justify the return on marketing investment (ROMI). In other situations, marketing departments are structured around the product, and business groups and resources are minimized for corporate functions. This is especially true in consumer marketing because the brand (e.g., Tide detergent or Crest toothpaste) is more important than the corporate brand, which in this case, is Proctor & Gamble. While this is good for the development of new product roadmaps, it often falls short on really driving the levers of demand, especially in business-to-business (B2B) companies. Levers of demand are complicated. They require strategy, program development, and execution in a variety of geographies, with channels, partners, sales, and customers, depending on whether you are a B2B or B2C company.

Some companies have all of these functions. The problem is that they are often organized in a fragmented way, with chunks of marketing functions distributed to product divisions, regions, and partners. They are not managed in a holistic way. No wonder the function of marketing is challenging to manage. You would be hard-pressed to find similar fragmentation in other functions, such as R&D, finance, or manufacturing. Of course, there is the old adage that everyone is a marketer, both figuratively and literally. Who reading this chapter hasn't attended a meeting where the CFO or CEO thought he or she could write a better tag line than the marketing team?

To become more strategic, marketing departments need to be organized to deliver strategy and execution to both internal and external customers and be able to link and unify the customer touch points across the organization. Who else can do it? The successful implementation of marketing—from product conception (cradle) to obsolescence (grave)—requires functional competency, as well as a means of building collaboration and systems to improve the customer experience. In the July 2011 edition of *McKinsey Quarterly*, the authors suggest that customers engage companies and functions, such as sales or support, at a variety of touch points (product awareness, considerations, uses, etc.) and that many of these touch points are outside the function of marketing. According to the authors, "…a comprehensive strategy for engaging customers across them rarely emerges and, if one does, there's often no system for executing it or measuring its performance."

In some ways, the marketing function needs to be organized like a data network, with nodes, speed, interconnected systems, and data flow. As a result, I believe the most successful marketing organizations and leaders create and blend roles that drive business growth and deliver upon their functional objectives and deliverables. This is crucial to the role of marketing and CMO. So let me share something I have learned after being in the marketing function for over 25 years.

The more the marketing role is structured around deliverables and tactics, the less value the rest of the company (and the people who manage the budgets) will ascribe to the marketing function. In contrast, the greater the ability of marketing to influence the business—whether that be with strategy, value creation, new product development, or growth initiatives—the more value and importance a company will derive out of its marketing organization.

In my consulting practice and network, I have met many companies claiming enlightenment about the value of marketing. They say they want to build strategic marketing organizations, invest money, hire talented people, and so on. The goal, of course, is admirable. But then the tough questions are asked. You find out that the marketing department doesn't report to the CEO or president like the HR, finance, and operations departments do. Marketing reports two or three levels down in the organization. Is that a strategic investment in marketing? Ask another question, and they will tell you they don't know much about marketing. They read or were told by some consultant on the board that it is important, and they want to invest in it but watch it from a distance. "Prove to me that marketing has strategic value and we will elevate it in the organization," they pontificate.

In many cases, the marketing professionals who take on these roles are doomed to failure because their organizations are not really ready to engage or support the marketing function at an appropriate level or intensity. Finally, some sales-focused organizations, CEOs/owners and managers are not ready to be enlightened by a more capable and powerful marketing organization or leader. In fact, I would go out on a limb and tell marketers to be cautious when considering jobs where the leader runs both sales and marketing. I have seen so many marketing organizations be overwhelmed by the "tyranny of the current." What I mean by this is that the marketing function under sales is often reduced to short-term, tactical training, sales tools, and data sheets. In fact, where marketing reports to in the structure, be it the CEO, president, or sales leader, is a good barometer of how strategic the function is. Think about it. All of the key areas, such as the HR and finance departments, report to the CEO, yet the marketing department reports to an executive one level below?

So what roles make a marketing leader world class and increase the chances of success? After observing and managing great and not-so-great marketing organizations, I believe there are six key roles that most successful marketing organizations (and the leadership within them) play. Implementing them greatly improves the chances that world-class marketing will be delivered.

- **Be the Strategic Visionary for the Business** – Help the company and the board see what success in the future will look like to shape the company's direction. Be an externally facing PR/ Industry Analyst spokesperson, along with the CEO and other executives, to exuberantly evangelize this vision and strategy. In other words, set the business and strategy of the entity first, and run marketing second.

- **Grow Revenues and Shares While Effectively Managing Profitability** – Be the champion of growth in the company. Build strategic plans, portfolios, and initiatives that drive short-term growth and long-term revenue and market share while delivering on the bottom-line profits of the company (net profit, operating profit, EBIDA, etc.). Help the business extract more profit by recommending upsell products or changes in pricing or the marketing mix. In a survey conducted in Spencer Stuart's 9th annual CMO Summit, the top three marketing priorities were to drive top-line revenue growth, acquire new customers, and grow the market share.

- **Identify and Create New Business Opportunities** – Help the company identify new and adjacent business opportunities, which are market segments that can be grown organically or through acquisition. Assist the company with its decisions to make, buy, or build. Finally, lead the organization in the identification of potential partners or acquisition targets, if it is not growing organically.

- **Bring the Voice and Insights of Customers to CEO and C-Level Staff** – Do it in a way they can be internalized and used by the C-Suite to create value and a competitive advantage for the company.

  Listen to what customers and performance analytics are saying. Create different ways to interact with them and to capture that feedback (e.g., social media). Be able to aggregate the data and provide meaningful insights that are credible and actionable.

- **Create and Manage the Right Marketing Structures** – Be able to successfully brand, create, introduce, manage, and sell a company's products and services at the appropriate cost and with the right return on investment. Not everything in marketing is fun and glamorous. There is a need to create structures that measure the marketing investment return of the money we spend, and to create structures and processes to get what we need out of the organization to deliver the functional goals. In addition, we also need to be skilled in the functional practice of creative and innovative marketing and understand and master relevant, new marketing techniques and practices as they evolve. The afore-mentioned Spencer Stuart survey identified 1) metrics and analytics, 2) social media, and 3) digital strategy as the marketing capabilities needed to build or add to the company's marketing strategy and priorities.

- **The Proper Role of Marketing is a Blend of Activities and Roles Over the Strategic Planning Horizon -** Spend too much time in strategic planning, and the company may view marketing as being in an ivory tower. Spend too much time in tactical execution mode, however, and marketing might not be seen as a value-added strategic function, but as one that wildly spends money on frivolous activities—the classic Prisoner's Dilemma. While not easy, good marketing organizations are able to balance the two very well. One other thing I would mention is that, as a functional marketing leader, spending either too much time in strategy or execution, risks you being labeled as too strategic (can't execute) or not strategic enough. A Zen-like balance and harmony on this continuum is crucial. It is reminiscent of a classic story:

A student asked a Zen Master,'If I work very hard, how long will it take for me to realize Zen?'
The Master replied,
'Ten years.'

The student replied,
"If I work very, very hard,
how long will it take for me to realize Zen?"
The Master replied,
"Twenty years."

The student replied,
"If I work very, very, very hard,
how long will it take for me to realize Zen?"

The Master replied,
"Thirty years."

The student replied,
"But I don't understand.
Why does it take longer when I work harder?"
The Master replied,
"When you have one eye on the goal, you only have one eye on
the path."

Too often in marketing we are obsessed with the goal, to the point that we
fail to understand that the path or the process we used to reach the goal is
equally, if not sometimes more, important.

In summary, marketing is the only function within the office of the
CEO that can broadly lead an organization down the path of growth and
strategic insight. This function touches the whole organization, from
product conception to the end of life. Because of the scope of what
marketing people do, this leadership does not and cannot come from
other areas, such as HR, finance, or operations functions. The secret
to successful marketing leadership is to be grounded in the business,
execute the six key roles, and focus everything on growing the business
and enabling the sale force, channels, and partners to be successful at
selling more products. Because marketing is constantly changing, the
mix of capabilities and skills is changing as well. Marketing leaders
who stay abreast and adapt to these changes are more likely to have a
longer tenure in the C-Suite.

## About Vince

Vince Ferraro is a general management executive and VP of Global Strategy and Marketing for Kodak's Consumer Digital Group and Corporate Marketing. As the marketing leader for one of the most iconic, recognized brands in the world, he is responsible for branding, advertising, communications, PR, social media, Kodak.com, and the e-commerce store. He also provides oversight and marketing leadership to Consumer Business, which includes product categories such as digital and video cameras, scanners, picture kiosks, and inkjet printers. He joined Kodak in November 2010 and also served as Vice President of Global Marketing for Kodak's Digital Printing Solutions Group. He was previously Vice President of Global Marketing for Hewlett-Packard's LaserJet business unit, where he was responsible for development and launch of some of the most successful and iconic technology products in the world.

Mr. Ferraro has over 25 years of experience building, managing, and growing a variety of lines of high technology hardware, consumables, and software businesses both domestically and internationally. In previous roles, Ferraro was VP of Marketing for HP's Business and Imaging group and HP's consumer businesses, which included digital cameras, photo printers, scanners, and DeskJet-, Photosmart-, and OfficeJet-branded products. He developed HP's first Windows- and Mac-compatible color inkjet printers—the PaintJet and PaintWriter product lines—and helped establish HP's wide-format plotter business with the introduction of the 7600 Series product line.

Other executive and management positions that he has occupied include international and regional senior roles in marketing, finance, and category business management functions.

Mr. Ferraro is also a social media pioneer, having established HP's most successful executive blog, which was quoted in the book "Groundswell: Winning in a World Transformed by Social Technologies" and was an Ad Age Power 150 blog. He is currently the author of the Tech Marketing Peitho blog (www.techmarketingpeitho.com).

Mr. Ferraro has received a B.S. in business administration (cum laude) from San Diego State University and a M.B.A. from the W.P. Carey School of Business at Arizona State University. He is also a graduate of Stanford University's Strategic Marketing Management Program. Mr. Ferraro has consulted with a variety of nonprofits, established businesses, and start-ups to increase the effectiveness of their business strategies and marketing plans. He sits on the North American Board of Advisors for the CMO Council and is a domain expert in the Connect Springboard Program.

Mr. Ferraro is a frequent speaker at such groups as the Silicon Valley Venture Capital Association, the CMO Council, Lyra, and various business networking groups and other industry events. He also speaks on technology marketing topics and how to utilize social media, such as LinkedIn, to its best advantage, and help others find new employment opportunities and create and deliver their own world-class personal brands.

Learn more about Vince at his website at: www.vincentferarro.com.

CHAPTER 9

# How To Win Like A Big Business By Focusing On Inbound Marketing
## - With Killer Online Marketing Strategies

By Paddu Govindaraj

Rewind to the eighties and nineties. Recollect how businesses operated. If you wanted to be successful and grow the business to even a reasonable size, you had to be big. You had to be really big - with tons of resources in terms of capital investment, human resources, marketing budget, great publicity machine and even bigger marketing machinery to feed the press, television and radio – in real terms.

If you did not have any of these ingredients, your small business will be an also-ran, with minimal income to sustain you or your small team and your maximum efforts as inputs. Your only option was to insert an advertisement in the Yellow Pages and hope that your telephone rings! Probably it is not much better than having a stable job in a large, well-known organization.

Fast forward to 2010 and think about the freedom gained by small businesses in terms of marketing reach. Your imagination is the limit. You do not need an army of people and millions of dollars to take on or even beat the big guys in the industry. Traditional marketing channels are undergoing a slow death. And online marketing is opening a great opportunity for small business owners and entrepreneurs.

This phenomenon is not unique to America and other developed nations. It is taking root even in under-developed and developing countries around the world.

Your marketing and sales efforts can now be measured and tracked to a great extent. You can spend a few hundred dollars on Google (pay per click marketing) and track the results precisely. If it does not produce results, you can tweak your tactics and change your strategies. You do not need to sign a contract for a hundred thousand dollars or print 10,000 brochures for the Tradeshow that you are attending for first time.

Your website and other online media is the front-end for most small businesses. The customers cannot differentiate between you – the small business owner – and the army of marketing wizards at big corporations. Rather, they don't care about your size, if you provide the services as promised on your online media. In fact, they will like you more because of your quick service and flexibility in your nimble business operations.

## LEVERAGE THE INTERNET AS A BUSINESS DRIVER

Internet has brought unlimited opportunities for small business owners. Information, knowledge and access to technology are key drivers of business growth in this information era. Over 70 percent of American consumers use the internet for research before taking a buying decision.

Whether you are in a soft business such as software, consulting, insurance services or real estate sales, or in a hard-core business such as plumbing, dentistry, automotive services, and home improvement and remodeling services, you can and should leverage the Internet and online marketing. Not only can you compete with established and traditional businesses, but you can also be more successful.

## EMBRACE INBOUND MARKETING AND KICK OUT OUTBOUND MARKETING

Inbound Marketing refers to the process of attracting prospective customers through online marketing channels such as websites, blogs, online videos, search engines, online directories and social media venues.

Visualize the process of prospects reaching your sales funnel via Google search. They have taken pains to research online and got attracted to your promise of quality products or services as portrayed on your online channels. Compare this process with the traditional outbound sales processes such as telemarketing, list chasing or Yellow Pages advertising – where you know nothing about the prospects and they know nothing about your organization.

Also, unlike traditional marketing practices, inbound marketing processes are highly scalable and the results are measurable to a maximum extent.

## USE SOCIAL MEDIA AS A BUSINESS CATALYST

Mass adoption of social media tools such as Twitter, LinkedIn, Facebook and GooglePlus has resulted in a number of opportunities for small businesses and professionals aspiring to be entrepreneurs.

While the large businesses with their bureaucratic processes and hierarchical organization structures struggle to understand the new online marketing channels and gather speed, smart and small businesses exploit the opportunities and grow in an exponential manner.

To be successful in the social media world, you need to be smart, but do not need the brute force that big businesses have!

## PERSONAL BRANDING IS KEY FOR SMALL BUSINESS OWNERS

Many small business owners and marketers are scared of online, Internet-based marketing.

Whether you are a consultant, plumber, author, or a landscaping service provider, you become the 'brand' and face of your business. Your expertise, authority and domain knowledge builds the online reputation of your business. Your business should be visible 24/7 online to your potential customers.

I am sure that all of us have dealt with real estate agents and insurance sales professionals. Why do you think that many of them put their photos and include their mobile phone number on their business card? They, as a personal 'brand' are ready to engage us any time we need help.

Small business owners and marketers putting their personal and team profiles and contact information online is no different to the above practice!

Also, take advantage of tools such as free eBooks and online videos to reach your target audience in cyber space and increase personal brand visibility. Establish yourself as an authority in your line of business by showcasing your subject matter expertise.

## TEN KEYS TO WIN CUSTOMERS

Here is a summary of ten keys to win customers and succeed big in small business.

- Establish your online presence and reputation with blogs, social media and online video tools. Your hesitation to do so will delay your success.

- Become a subject matter expert in your domain by sharing free information and knowledge useful to your prospective customers.

- Increase your online visibility by going to the online locations where your prospects are likely to hangout and engage with them in meaningful conversations. These could be blogs, forums, LinkedIn groups, or Twitter channels.

- Leverage multiple sources for lead generation. Never depend on one avenue as the lead source, which is not only risky but you will be missing out on a lot of potential up for grabs in other avenues.

- Keep up with the technology developments and adapt quickly. Technology is a key business driver and do not treat it as a necessary evil or an accessory.

- Be ready to tap into the mobile technology revolution unfolding currently. Smart phones and tablets will change the consumer behavior significantly. Mobile technologies will disrupt the online marketing space, will drive more and more consumers online and demand major changes in how businesses will operate in future.

- Be prepared to engage and service prospects over weekends and evenings, as consumer behavior and buying patterns change. There are no 'after hours' in online buying and eCommerce. You can get help at a reasonable cost to handle these customer engagement activities.

- Use online software tools and systems for lead generation and capture, follow-up and conversion activities. Do not depend on manual or semi-automatic processes where the activities can be fully automated.

- Customer expectations and technology changes are witnessing exponential growth. Be nimble and take this as an opportunity to identify new business avenues!

- Be active and visible in localized online marketing channels. Yelp, Google Places and online directories are great tools to increase visibility in this area.

The key advantage to being a small business is that customers do not expect you to spend extraordinary efforts and money for online marketing.

For example, customers expect big businesses to provide quality videos online. As a small business, you can get away with ordinary, low quality videos – they expect it to be useful with the right information, but do not bother about the format and quality in which it is delivered.

In other words, customers care about function rather than form when dealing with a small business. As long as you deliver good, useful and relevant content, they would be happy to engage with and buy from you.

## DO NOT FEAR THE TECHNOLOGY

Online marketing technology and jargon intimidate many small business owners. Do not fear the technology! In fact, most of the web technology and tools are based on pure common sense. And, unlike olden days, you do not need to spend tons of money and months of time to learn these so-called tricks and secrets of online marketing.

For instance, to learn about how to use Google Search Marketing (or PPC) for your business, you can fire up your browser and see what your peers are doing. You can see their website content, read their blogs and see where they hangout online. You can start with a ten dollar budget and start experimenting - which was unthinkable a decade ago. Most of this stuff is out in the open on the Internet. You need to sharpen your mind and focus.

Be wary of online courses and marketing programs offering to convert you to a marketing genius overnight! Some do add value and help you grasp the subject quickly. But most of those with lofty promises will be a mere waste of money.

## ONLINE LEAD GENERATION AND LEAD CONVERSION

To be successful in business, you must focus on lead generation as well as lead conversion. Many small business owners tend to ignore one or the other. Focusing on only one aspect of this equation will lead to wasted efforts and frustration.

Lead generation and conversion go hand in hand. This is more pronounced in the online marketing scenario. The prospects expect fast response for their online inquiry from the business. They also have more options and choices in the online world.

Hence, acquiring a lead from online sources does not end the sales process. Quick assessment, prompt follow up, and continuous engagement are requirements for getting leads converted to customers.

Also, keep in mind that social media tools help prospects and customers vent their frustration and anger if their inquiries are not handled or are mishandled. Small businesses should invest significant efforts in putting together tools and resources needed for staff involved in lead generation and conversion activities.

## CLOUD-BASED SOFTWARE TOOLS FOR MARKETING

Again, the cost of these tools is relatively low. With the invention of cloud-based software tools and services for lead capture, distribution to inside sales, automatic messaging and estimates, feedback, etc., the upfront investment in software and technology tools is almost nothing. This is another feature that small businesses should take advantage of.

As you generate more leads and revenue, the monthly service fees can be paid out of the earnings.

Cloud-based technologies have also resulted in significant reduction in technology maintenance and management for small businesses. In fact, the service providers force you to upgrade your knowledge and business practices as the technology and industry evolve.

For example, one of our customers in the lead generation industry requested a new feature in our LeadPro247 software. As one the heavy users of Pay Per Click marketing, they were losing significant amounts of money in terms of wasted leads. The leads are provided to their customers in real time. If there are no pending customer orders for a specific type of lead at a particular point in time, the leads generated with PPC advertising will go waste. Obviously, the prospects will also get frustrated as no one would be following up with them, though they have submitted their contact information and were expecting a quick response.

Hence, our customer requested that we establish a process to hook up with Google and MSN, and turn off the PPC advertisements, if there are no customers in the lead system. We provided the new feature and deployed it to our cloud-based software service. The customer estimated that there was a saving of 10% to 15% by using this new feature. Once it proved useful, we made the feature available to our other customers without any additional fees.

This practice is common among the cloud-based service providers and is a major reason why these subscription-based services are quickly adopted by small business users.

## HAPPY SELLING!

The definition of marketing and sales has undergone a sea of change with the popularity of online marketing. Grab this opportunity and win big.

If you think that a depressed economy is an issue to start new online marketing initiatives or business ventures at this juncture, think twice. Customers are expecting more value at lower prices in order to manage their day to day life. Online marketing saves money, enables better decision-making by providing quality information about the products and services being sold to them, and increases customer engagement.

Tools such as online surveys and pay per click marketing enable small businesses to reach and engage the right audience and experiment with various marketing options. Hence, there is no reason to lie low and let the opportunity pass by. Think and act like a big business and take them head on. You are *In It To Win It*. Happy selling!

## About Paddu

Paddu Govindaraj is an inbound marketing and sales strategy expert with over two decades of technology experience. He specializes in strategies and best practices for online lead generation, lead conversion, customer relationship management and loyalty management.

Paddu is a serial entrepreneur and launched several marketing and technology start-ups in North America and Asia. He is the founder of LeadPro247, a leading online lead generation, and distribution and management software and service provider. LeadPro247 is a leading service provider for online Publishers, Affiliates, Advertisers, Media agencies, Lead generation and sales organizations.

He is an expert in the online lead generation domain. He provides consulting services to Fortune 500 companies, small and medium-sized businesses and online media agencies on best practices in online marketing, marketing automation, lead generation, enterprise sales and lead conversion.

Paddu helps tiny, small and medium-sized businesses transition from traditional marketing practices to Internet and Social Media-based marketing. He mentors small business owners and marketers to standout from the crowd in the online marketing world.

He is also the author and publisher of several blogs in the lead generation, search engine marketing and online survey research areas. He is well known in the industry and participates in online seminars and industry conferences as a blogger, panelist and presenter.

Paddu holds a Masters degree in Information Systems and Marketing, in addition to a degree in Science. He has also worked on marketing, sales and customer management technology projects with large corporate organizations such as Owens Corning, Tata Group and Ford Motor Company on major marketing systems initiatives. He has managed enterprise-wide CRM and ERP systems implementation projects.

He actively participates in several entrepreneurial and technology startup accelerator organizations.

To lead more about Paddu Govindaraj and his services, you can connect with him on Twitter at: http://www.Twitter.com/PadduG or visit:

http://www.PadduGovindaraj.com.

If you are managing Internet lead generation, distribution and sales for your organization, you may request a thirty day trial for the LeadPro247 lead distribution and management system by visiting: http://www.LeadPro247.com.

CHAPTER 10

# Making the Paradigm Shift to Success: Your Mindset Makes the Difference

By Gwendolyn Bridges

*"As iron sharpens iron, so one person sharpens another."*
~ Proverbs 27:17

Relationships, Careers, Lifestyles.... Everyone wants to find fulfillment in their life in the areas that matter most. But you don't see many *finding* that fulfillment.

So why is that? Why can't we get what we want out of life? Most of us go for the easy answer to that question - which is, there's something else out there that's to blame. Could be bad luck - or the economy - or other people getting in our way. You can always find a villain when you look hard enough. But when we put more effort into finding those villains rather than looking at ourselves...that gets us nowhere. It just makes all those bad bogeymen seem much more powerful - and makes us feel helpless to do anything against them.

There's no doubt that battling tough odds can mess up anyone's plans. But there is also no doubt that the most powerful success stories always involve overcoming those odds in order to achieve cherished goals.

Our biggest challenges come not from outside circumstances, but from our own internal outlooks. How we view ourselves, our lives and the people we encounter on a day-to-day basis can either take us down the road to a satisfying and productive life, or leave us at a frustrating and debilitating dead end. Our attitudes can either open doors or cause them to be closed in our faces.

We can't be "*in it to win it*" without the right mindset. To make it to that mindset, we often require a "paradigm shift" - which means an across-the-board change in the basic assumptions that you use in your everyday life. So let's talk about how you can make that shift - and make a better life for you and the ones you love.

## THE CHANGE IS IN YOU

That timeworn expression, "You can't teach an old dog new tricks," certainly gets a workout. You hear those words and you think to yourself, "Well, there's no point in trying to be different. I'm an adult, I am what I am, and that's all there is to it."

That's the kind of mindset that will stop you in your tracks - I mean *completely*. When you have that mindset in place, it means you're settling for where you are right now for the rest of your life. You've closed yourself off to many great and wonderful possibilities - because you've just told yourself, "Nope, can't do it."

But you can. Anyone can - if they're willing to do what it takes. And someone I find inspirational who *proves* it can be done is a woman named Ernestine Shepherd. Now, when Ernestine made it to the age of 56, those who knew her thought she was the last person on earth that would end up doing anything differently with her life. She was a school secretary who wasn't in the greatest shape - she wasn't physically active (she herself described herself as a "slug"), and her body shape reflected that.

Then one day, she went bathing suit shopping with her sister – both of whom had been beautiful girls. In the changing room, while trying different suits on, they got a good look at where they were now - and ended up laughing at how badly out-of-shape they were. So, they both joined a gym and started working out.

Tragically, a few months later, her sister died suddenly and unexpectedly from a brain aneurysm. Ernestine was, naturally, devastated - and stopped going to the gym, because she no longer had anyone to go with. But, after a few months, she realized her sister would have wanted her to keep going and continue what they started.

That woman soon experienced her own major paradigm shift. As she transformed her body and got it into the best condition of her life, she also transformed her attitude and found fulfillment in an entirely new career that even she could never have seen coming - as a female bodybuilder and athlete.

Now, at the age of 74, this remarkable lady has completed nine marathons and won two bodybuilding competitions. Not only that, but she has made a place for herself in the Guinness Book of World Records as the oldest competitive female bodybuilder in the world (she didn't enter her first contest until she was 71!).

As Ernestine likes to say, "Age is nothing but a number." It's never too late. How old you are does not predict or predicate change - your mind is in control of making that happen. And the moment you make the decision to change, you make a whole new life for yourself.

## MY PERSONAL JOURNEY

My career has been incredibly important to me - but my personal development has been just as big a priority. I am incredibly motivated to live the best life I can. Much of that motivation comes from the person I call the guiding force in my life, my beautiful daughter Jazmyn, who is 23 years old as I write this. She recently received her Bachelor of Science Degree in Sports Management from Howard University and is now pursuing her Masters at the University of San Francisco.

To stimulate my personal growth, I've done boot camps and seminars, I've journaled, and I've read life-changing books like Dale Carnegie's "How to Win Friends and Influence People." I've learned from such motivational leaders as Tony Robbins, Dani Johnson, Jack Canfield and most recently, the man whose name appears on the front cover of this book, Tom Hopkins. I've taken the skills I've learned from these great people and applied them to my personal and professional lives. And it's made some kind of difference.

All this wisdom has taught me to raise the bar each time I attempt a new challenge in my life - to truly be "in it to win it." If you put that message out to the universe, the universe will reward you. For sure, I was a little nervous to participate in this book - to put in the time, make the investment and, maybe most of all, put my thoughts out there for the whole world to see.

But I decided this was an important part of my own paradigm shift - to share what I've learned over a lifetime and maybe enable people reading this to create the change they've been looking for in their own lives. I believe that when you teach what you yourself have learned, that is when you become a true master.

## THE SHIFT STARTS WITH PEOPLE

One of the things you really have to look at when you think about making a change is your associations - the people you surround yourself with. Good associations can make or break your deal. When Quentin Groves, a player for the Oakland Raiders, was a kid, he had five close friends that he hung out with. They got into some trouble and he ended up in Juvenile Hall.

While he was there, he had some time to think - and realized that those friends were leading him in the wrong direction. That was the basis of a big paradigm shift. He stopped being friends with those danger-seeking boys, got himself on a better track and he excelled. Now, of course, he's made a great career for himself in the NFL.

By the same token, there are people you may have in your life that may not be helping you to reach your goals. As a matter of fact, they may be doing the opposite - they may be distracting you and cutting down on the amount of time you have to achieve what you want to achieve. We could be talking about family, friends, or business colleagues - whoever they are, if they're adding a negative influence to your life, you need to free yourself from that influence and find new associations that will enable you to fly high.

This is something I learned firsthand. As a matter of fact, I believe it took me about 35 years to really understand what the true definition of "friend" really is - and that's somebody who's in your corner and wants you to have what's best for you.

Phonies and those that are jealous of you aren't going to help you - and you can't really help them. That goes for your professional life as well as your personal life. As you go through your own paradigm shift, you should look to interact with the heavy hitters and successful entrepreneurs that can help you grow yourself into a major business.

Finally, when you have surrounded yourself with the right people and you do find that they've made a difference in your life, it's important to have an "attitude of gratitude." You must thank those who have helped you on your journey - and acknowledge the debt you owe them.

## STARTING YOUR JOURNEY

While it's important to surround yourself with the right people as you make your shift, the first person you really need to deal with is yourself. If you want people to follow your example and look up to you, you have to *be* that example first.

That starts with your mindset. Be proactive, not reactive - and listen to your subconscious - it knows what's best for you. When you "go by your gut" and trust your instincts, you follow a path that's already laid out for you. Your subconscious provides your guiding principle for an extraordinary life. Trust that guiding principle and it will take you to your passion and your fulfillment. Do the things you enjoy and you will be motivated to achieve.

Even though your guiding principle will lead you onward, you still need to make a concrete plan to reach your goals. As you create and work through that plan, know that you will hit obstacles you may not overcome at the moment and experience setbacks you had not expected. You are not alone! It's not the time to give up though - when you realize your plan needs an adjustment, you make it. Write down a new plan and make a checklist for getting things done.

And, whatever you do, don't let the past interfere with your future. You can't change what happened - but many have a hard time just moving on.

Sometimes people eat themselves up, dwelling on yesterday and hanging on to past wounds. If someone has hurt you, practice a forgiving heart and try to get an understanding of that person's side. Don't be so much of a talker, be a listener and attempt to really understand what happened. You may experience a paradigm shift in your relationship with that person!

You also want to possess a presentation of physical excellence. Your outward appearance represents who you are. If you don't look healthy, people will react to you differently. You don't have to be a champion bodybuilder like Ernestine, but health and fitness *are* important! Some people beat themselves up and tell themselves that they're just losers - and the next thing that happens is they pound down a bunch of donuts to make themselves feel better!

I still recall when former President Bill Clinton used to jog by (and into) McDonalds - and a few years later, had to have extensive heart surgery. I asked myself, "How can a man control the United States government - and not control himself?" It's a question people will ask about you if you don't keep yourself in decent physical shape. When you eat well and exercise, it does reflect that you have a high self-worth and it will, in fact, make you feel better about yourself.

Tend to your spiritual health as well as your physical health too. If your inner belief is a beautiful thing, everyone will see that beauty in you. Choose wise counsel that will feed your spirit and nourish your heart. Keep in mind, you don't have to meet these people in person to soak in their knowledge and advice. The personal mentors I listed earlier all have many books and videos available to learn from. The resources are out there - you just have to make use of them, and then, most importantly, actually find the relevant ways to apply their content to your life.

Don't let your head get lost in the clouds, though. Keep it real and be yourself. Be honest and trustworthy. And have an open mind to new concepts and ideas. When you close yourself off to new wisdom and new experiences, you close yourself off to growth. If you act like you've already arrived, how can anyone help you to the next level? People can be destroyed by ignorance - just because they reject knowledge. If you're willing to sit down and get educated, you open up the doors to personal progress and professional success.

That education definitely should extend to how to handle money. There are folks who have the ability to earn big - but they may not have developed the financial literacy that allows them to build those paydays into growth for the future, as well as to establish a legacy that aids their children and grandchildren. This is the field I am working in now, to help people prepare for such financial challenges as retirement and college tuition for their kids, and it is incredibly gratifying.

## 7 ACTION STEPS TOWARDS YOUR GOALS

So what do you want to get out of life? It's there for the taking - if you're willing to do what it takes to reach your goals. Here are seven simple "Action Steps" I suggest that will guide you on your way.

1. **Build on your natural talents** - God will take care of the rest!

2. **Never do it just for the money** - do it instead for the joy and the wonderful feeling you get while you're doing it!

3. **Stay focused on serving** - when you serve others well, the universe has a way of handling everything else.

4. **Be proactive** - initiate, lead, go fast and step out on stage.

5. **Keep a smile in your heart** - be genuine, honest, open-minded, patient and understanding.

6. **Find a mentor or coach** - and be coachable and teachable when you do find the right person.

7. **Get knowledge and apply it** - use what you learn to take you to the next level.

I wish you much success on your journey - and hope that we can cross paths someday to share our knowledge and life lessons.

## About Gwendolyn

"He is the Source of my strength and
the strength of my life."

As an entrepreneur, personal life coach, motivational speaker, and now author, Gwendolyn Bridges is using her God-given talents to help others make a change in their life for success.

Gwendolyn is a dynamic and creative professional, with strengths in people management, operational management, sales, marketing and client relations. Experienced in establishing and managing customer and sales operations, promotions and program management. She has been acknowledged for excellent communication skills, leadership, integrity and working with a high level of initiative. Through personal development and learned skills she reaches out to all that she can to help them take and complete the necessary steps towards reaching their goals.

Gwendolyn currently resides in Northern California with her loving daughter Jazmyn.

# CHAPTER 11

# GETTING ON GOOGLE

## By Adam Robinson

Optimizing your website for internet exposure is called Search Engine Optimization, or SEO. The goal of most websites is to achieve a premium ranking on Google for the site's relevant search terms or "key words." If the site ranks highly with Google, chances are that it will do equally well on other sites such as Yahoo, Bing, Ask, and numerous others. To achieve a high-ranking site you need SEO. A common goal is to be listed on the first page. Rarely do users go past two or three pages and many don't go past the first page.

The first thing to choose is the site's purpose and (domain) name. I suggest that you do not try to be vague or cover an entire industry/product. The more targeted your site is to a niche market, the easier it will be to rank. Remember you can have more than one site. You can build many different sites to sell to many "niche" markets. For example, if you sell "widgets," it will be much easier to obtain ranking for "luxury small plastic blue widgets made in the USA" than just the term "widgets." Also, a relevant domain name will be easier to obtain for a more specific product. Decide exactly what your primary product or market is, then go after that market. After you dominate in your first market or product, then dominate the next on your list. The second one will be easier than the first.

SEO, or search engine optimization, is a complete industry. There are many companies trying to sell SEO services, some more reputable than others. SEO can be done in two ways, "white hat" SEO and "black hat" SEO. White hat is following the rules and doing things correctly, whereas black hat tries to cheat by breaking the rules. Be very cautious, Google is very smart and eventually catches the cheaters. The penalty is being "black listed" or completely removed from Google. Of course, there is always something in between black and white called "grey." Again, be careful, not just of what you do, but who you hire other's to do it.

SEO can be divided into two types of work that can be done to achieve a higher ranking for web sites, onsite and off site. First there is onsite work, content on the site itself. An authority site needs to have fresh content that is updated frequently. The most important thing to remember is that that site will never be completed. The site will always need to be updated. Consider your website a magazine that has new content published on a regular basis. It is not a book that is written and completed. A static site that is not updated will eventually not rank well. A good plan is to add a new page of content to your site each week. At the end of a year you will have added 50 pages to your site.

There are several basic items you need to know about for your site. First, know your search phrases or key words. These are relevant terms people use to search for your product. Google offers an entire site on how to determine how many searches are done for any term or phrase at https://adwords.google.com. This site has several tools that will be helpful in optimizing your site. The Google "keyword" tool will suggest key words for you to use and show you how often each keyword is searched for each month. This is easy to use and the free information is provided directly from Google.

The more detailed the search phrase, the more targeted the visitor will be.

It will be much easier to rank well for "long tail" key words than short ones.

To achieve a first page ranking for "widgets" will be more difficult than ranking for long term key words "small plastic blue widget" Start by composing a list of keywords that you would like your site to rank for. For each key word build a page, going into detailed information on that keyword. Each page should have a title, a meta tag, header, and title tag, all containing that keyword phrase. This sounds like a lot of work but when done over time it will become easier and routine. Your site needs to be simple enough to use so that you can update it yourself or at least update it in-house. Your site needs a site map and it should be submitted to Google on a regular basis. This is something that you might need a Webmaster to build for you. However, you should have the ability to add pages, photos, and other content to your site yourself.

To be a top-ranking site, the site should be the content authority in it's subject. The site should feature more pages of information and current content about your product than your competitor's sites. If you are selling widgets, then there should be pages on every size widget, every color of widget, every material, domestic widgets, imported widgets, etc. Good quality content is most important. While you want to use your key words in your content, do not "stuff" them onto pages and use them unnecessarily. There are several ways to add content to your site. You can add pages of text, photos or images, and now video. A blog is good way to discuss news about your site. *A good idea is to add new content on a regular basis.*

Perhaps every Monday add a new web page, every Tuesday a video, every Wednesday a blog, every Thursday a slide show of photos, and on Friday a special offer or event.

At the end of the year, your site will most likely rank on the first page of Google for your product. Always keep your keywords and target audience in mind. Use your keywords frequently but naturally in articles, titles, blogs, graphs and photos. Remember to link internally on your site (from page to page) as well as to begin to create relevant external links (links to other sites).

If your site is an authority on its product or subject, then it is natural that other sites would link to it. These are called back links. Google (and other search engines) look for this by using electronic spiders. They spider all sites to see who is linking to your site. A site with many back links will rank higher than a site without back links. Getting other sites to link to your site is off site SEO. You can pay someone to back link to your site, or you can buy back links by the hundreds this is called black hat SEO. Be very careful about who you hire and who they pay to back link to your site. When caught, your site could be "black listed" and removed from the search engine completely. If your goal is to have a long-term authority site, don't do it. However, you can encourage others to link to your site by providing relevant content that the users of their site would naturally find informational. The key is to keep these back links natural. Google is very good at recognizing and banning paid back links. If your site has never been linked to by another site, then all of a sudden 500 sites link to it in two weeks, Google will most likely know you're doing something unethical.

There are many ways to get lots of links to your site without buying them. Perhaps you can offer to exchange links with someone in your industry in another area, or do a guest blog on another site in a different industry in your area. Offer to provide a tool which updates your product on another site. A good example of this would be the "weather" information snippet provided by weather or news stations on sites in their service areas. Or if you are a mortgage broker, provide mortgage rate information to a number of real estate web sites. This can generate lots of traffic and better rankings. Commenting on other blogs and social media is also a good method of back linking. If a thousand people "like" your blog, then Google will notice (even better if a million people "like" it). Videos uploaded to YouTube are a great method of getting traffic to your web site. Having video is an important part of SEO. For many products there are almost as many YouTube searches as there are Google searches. If you don't know this, Google owns YouTube. Also, YouTube creates text for the audio on their videos, so audio on a video is just as important as words are on a page.

Another method to create traffic and back links is by submitting your site to directories —and in particular to the Yahoo Directory. These are becoming less important and less effective, but are still good ways to build your site's ranking on Google.

To summarize, it is important to always be working on your internet presence. Never think your site is completed. Every week add new relevant content, a new page each week works, then promote that content with blogs, videos and links from other sites.

## About Adam

Since 1989, Internet marketing pioneer Adam Robinson, has been selling real estate in Southwest Florida. As the Internet evolved, he realized that online marketing would transform business and become a Realtors'® primary marketing tool for selling real estate. Adam realized that even a state of the art website is only as valuable as the traffic it receives, and the leads it generates. His mission became to master the knowledge of search engine optimization and search engine marketing. Strategies include site architecture optimization, content optimization, meta tag optimization, free and paid link-building and much more.

In 2005, after working for and owning several national franchises, Adam opened his own real estate firm. With his wealth of information and motivating advice, he is able to hand-pick the agents who share his passion for combining high technology with personal service.

Describing his business philosophy, Robinson recently commented:—
"Our systems are constantly improving each year. I am eager to learn what other Internet marketing pioneers in the country are using, and to adapt the most successful systems to the real estate business. For our agents, we strive to successfully optimize their personal and business websites with the goal of getting them more traffic, and ultimately, more clients. These skills earn our agents hundreds of thousands of dollars each year. With constant improvements, our systems continue to be highly efficient in selling our agents' listings, as well as in locating homes for our agents' clients. I feel that when the market gets more difficult, it opens up an amazing opportunity to gain market share. In real estate, you must always be improving and delivering the highest service possible to your agents in order to be successful.

"You not only have to provide the absolute best service to survive in this industry, but you must also net your agents more money."

CHAPTER 12

# How to Get People to Like You

## By John Sullivan

I know you probably heard that people buy from people they like, but it's true! How do you get a stranger to like you? I found that early in my selling career, there are potential clients that I bonded with and others not so much. Just like life, I guess. My first sales job was with a computer systems company where I would be their only salesperson. We had a tele-marketer who would get an equipment list from a company; we would then price it and send it back. If they liked the price, I get a meeting, if not, nothing. As you can imagine, things didn't always go well. My sales manager, so to speak, was the President of the company with no sales experience. His pep talk was he would look me in the eye, give a 'thumbs up' and say, "Hang in there!" I realized that I needed help and sought out sales training.

I went to see the best, including Tom Hopkins, Tony Robbins and Brian Tracy, to name a few. Through them and on my own, I came up with what I think are nine principals of getting people to like you and trust you. They are Rapport, Questions, Hand Shake, Match and Mirroring, Agreeing With Them, 3rd partying it, Don't be pushy, Gifts, and Thank You Notes. Let's go through each one:

## 1. Rapport

Rapport is the most important aspect of selling followed closely by questions. Think about it, don't you bond with people that you have things in common with? It's that synergy that draws you to people. If you don't have rapport with your prospect, you're probably not going to get the sale. You need to find a commonality with that person. You need for them to say, "I like this person, I trust this person." As I said before, sometimes it just comes naturally, other times it doesn't. It's those other times that you need to change in order to be a successful sales person. Customers always want to know what's in it for them. They also love to talk about themselves. Most salespeople are talking about THEIR Company, THEIR product.

## 2. Questions

You need to get to know your prospect. You must ask several opening questions to get the prospect talking. They are Past, Present & Future questions. Past: How long have you been with the company or how did you get this position? Present: How many employees work for you or work here? Future: Where do you see yourself in 5, 10 years? This gets the prospect to talk about themselves! As I mentioned before, questions are a close second to the most important aspect of selling. Questions have YOU in control of the meeting. Open-ended questions force your prospect to start talking. This way you are now able to take your prospect down the path of them buying from you Isn't, ...

"Who is servicing your equipment now?"

"What do you like about your service company?"

"If you could improve their service, how would you do it?"

"Who other than yourself makes the decision on service contracts?"

...a lot better than... "ABC Company has been in business for ......" Blah, Blah, Blah.

Questions get your prospect talking about them. What their problems are, what would motivate them to buy your product or service? If you are doing most of the talking you are probably not going to get the sale unless your prospect desperately needs your product or service. In a selling situation, whoever talks the most loses! I always thought that you had to dominate the conversation in a sales call until I found out it doesn't work most of the time, and questions have a much easier way to get the sale in the end.

## 3. The Handshake

Your handshake is one of the first ways your prospect judges you. Before he decides if he wants your product or service or if he is going like you, the handshake starts things off. When you first approach your prospect look him or her in the eyes, smile and shake their hand. Make sure the web of your hand is aligned with their web and grip their hand with the same pressure as they give you. Don't go in for the death grip and try to show him what a rugged individual you are. They will probably think "Oh boy, another pushy salesperson." Also don't give the prospect a wimpy handshake either; you want to have your prospect respect you. If they come in hard or soft, apply the same pressure. I know this sounds crazy, but you need to practice this so you can change your grip pressure quickly to their grip pressure, when first shaking hands.

## 4. Match and Mirroring

Statistics say that the degree of influence is broken down by the following: Words are 7%, Tonality 38% and Body Language is 55%!

When you are in front of a prospect, you need to match and mirror their movements. If your client is sitting up straight, you must sit up straight. If they have their arms folded, you must fold your arms. If they are speaking at a fast pace you must do the same. You must do it in subtle movements. Don't move your hand as soon as they do it. Wait a few moments and then mirror the movement. After doing this for a while, it is time to see if rapport is being built. You now make a gesture and see if your prospect follows. I like to either sit up if I'm sitting back or sit back if I was sitting up. If your prospect follows your movement, you're in business. Keep doing it until you and your prospect are aligned.

Some people may be uncomfortable with matching and mirroring another person, and they feel like it is manipulative. Just realize that it is part of the rapport building process and you are doing it all the time anyway. You are doing it with your family and friends. Do you ever notice a couple act and talk the same way, or their children have the same mannerisms? If you have never done this, then practice it with someone. Have a conversation with another person and don't tell them what you're doing. Watch what happens!

## 5. Agreeing with them

When you are in a discussion or giving your presentation with your prospect don't fight their objections. You must always agree with them and then ask a question. If you are selling real estate for a living and your client says, "I heard this school district isn't very good"... you can say, "That's a good question, where did you hear that?" ...and you get them to elaborate. They might say, "My brother-in-law's sister who lives 100 miles away heard!" They would probably dismiss it at that point. You can't say to them, "Oh that's not true at all, it's one of the best school districts in the state." That's why you need to ask a question to get them to confirm their issue. If you are dealing with two people in a presentation (Husband and Wife for example), when an objection comes up, pause for a second because the other person might answer the objection for you. You would then agree with them. Remember if you say it it's doubtful. If they say it, it's true!

Even during the presentations, if your prospect makes an observation, always commend them. "That's a good point" or "Thanks for mentioning that." There are a lot of other examples for agreeing with them and then asking a question, but that would be a chapter in itself.

## 6. 3rd Partying It

Another way of handling questions and building rapport is by 3rd partying it. This is when a prospect has an objection and you handle it by deferring it to another person or company. For example: your prospect says, "I'm a little nervous about investing in mutual funds." You agree with them, don't fight them or tell them how wrong they are. "I know what you mean; Peter (their neighbor, friend, anyone or any company they know) felt the same way. But after investing in them through us, he has seen great results. Does that help?" or "I never used another company besides the manufacturer before." "I know how you feel, ABC company (a name they know) felt the same way you do, but after using us for over three years now, they absolutely love our service." You see how 3rd partying IT softens the blow? You're not saying it, ABC company says it.

## 7. Don't Be Pushy

Nobody likes a pushy salesperson and everybody has come face-to-face with one. When you mention the word salesman, people think of it as if you are using a curse word. Meanwhile, sales is probably the second oldest profession in history. I will let you draw your own conclusions what is first. The old school way of selling was telling the prospect what they need, using all sorts of closing techniques, then hound them until they sign. Only to have them probably cancel the order anyway. Nobody likes to get sold, but they love to buy. If you are being pushy, people will resist you. Did you ever walk into the store and the salesperson says, "Can I help you?" and your answer is, "No, I'm just looking." You are coming into the store for <u>something</u>, but it's a reaction answer. Instead, the non-pushy salesperson would say, "Hi my name is John, and if you need anything I will be over here." When the salesperson sees that the customer is over by the ____(let's say couches) he should ask an involvement question. "Are you going to be using the couch for your living room or den?" Either answer is good because the customer is now telling you that they have a need. With the pushy way, you are getting nowhere. Using the soft way, you are now engaged with the prospect.

## 8. Gifts

A gift can be a touchy subject unless it's done casually. When you give someone something, they feel the need to give you something back. It's called the "Law of Reciprocity." Robert Cialdini, author of The Psychology of Persuasion says, "it's the rule that we should try to repay, in kind, what another person has provided for us." He tells of the story of the Hare Krishna, and how they would dress in robes and sandals and chant in the airports and try to collect money from people. They used the Law of Reciprocity by giving people little flowers and in turn ask for a donation. They made a lot of money. They were successful because people were receiving the flowers so they felt the need to give something back. After a while people were expecting them, so when the Krishnas would give a flower the suspecting people would not take it and let it hit the floor. Since the person did not take ownership of the gift, nothing was owed. The Krishnas were smart. They then would give out little American flags, and as Americans, we could not let them hit the ground! After a while people were able to avoid the Krishnas all together.

I'm not suggesting standing in airports giving out flowers, but there are less obvious ways to give a prospective customer a little token. One thing I like to do is give someone I visit a lottery ticket. I tell them that I just bought a few tickets and to take one. I just give it to them and say "here!" …very easy. Once the transaction takes place, I know they feel the need to reciprocate.

## 9. Thank You Notes

Thank you notes are one of the best ways for a potential customer to like you. I learned about thank you notes from Tom Hopkins 25 years ago. What a concept. After visiting with a customer, you send them a thank you note that's short and sweet. "Dear John, Thanks again for taking the time out to see me and it was a pleasure meeting you. We have been fortunate to serve many happy clients and I hope that we will do business together." It must be hand written as well, just like Tom says. Think about it, what's the first mail you open at home, bills, junk mail? Nope, hand written mail. My business requires a two-step sales call. I can't tell you how many times the customer mentioned the nice note I sent. Do you think he or she likes me? You bet! We now live in the electronic age and everything is sent via email. For them to get a hand written note is a terrific gesture and it gets noticed. People tell me they haven't received one of these in 30 years! What takes two minutes to write can get you tremendous rewards.

So there you go, **NINE** ways to get people to like you and trust you. Don't be afraid to use these tools. Practice them and make them your own like I did. Just imagine if one of these techniques work for you. I guarantee your income will soar.

## About John

### John V. Sullivan: Executive Vice President / Co Owner

John Sullivan is the Executive Vice President at Delta Computer Group. John has a long history of accomplishments in the industry, including being awarded IT Salesman of the Year and many other honors from various leading IT industry groups. Having joined Delta Computer Services in September 1997 after serving as Senior Vice President of Sales at US Computer Group for a decade, John Sullivan has reshaped Delta's sales force objective to focus on a consultative approach to the many IT needs of their customers. In addition to his vital role in leading the direction of Delta Computer Group sales team, John is committed to the continued development of Delta Computer Group's overall full service infrastructure.

Mr. Sullivan's overriding strategy to success is customer focus, and he insists that to maintain continued long term relationships and sales growth, Delta Computer Group must provide alert sensitivity to customer needs. He describes the philosophy in this way, "We must execute on the immediate needs of our customers, but at the same time develop long term strategies to ensure that our client's capabilities remain effective." It is this commitment to long term customer satisfaction and responsiveness that has fostered and realized the sales achievements of the Delta Computer Group.

# CHAPTER 13

# MY SECRETS TO SUCCESS

## By John Jochem

Michael Vance said management is not building cars through people. Management is building people through work – while making cars. Managers get paid for results and employees stay where they are growing: as people and financially. How do you manage salespeople for results and speed up the process? Tom Hopkins hired Michael Vance many years ago and achieved results. There are half-a-dozen things in any industry we must master for results. Find those half-a-dozen things first.

### THE 80/20 RULE

The 80/20 rule states 20% of your salespeople equal 80% of your production. 20% of your products equal 80% of your profit. Focus on the 20% which makes all of your money. Delete the 80% which hurts you or takes up your time. Focus on profit and results. Keep your eye on the prize.

The 80/20 rule states 20% of your products make 80% of your income. It is the job of managers to explain pay plans, motivate salespeople, and maximize profit with the 80/20 Rule. It is also manager's job to get the products, which can increase profit.

Why do you get paid as a manager? The answer is results. Just focus on the 20%. The answer could be sales, repeat sales or referrals. The business may depend on advertising. Managers get paid for results with as little conflict as possible. The 80/20 rule implies you should hire an assistant for your top producer and fire your lowest producer. The 80/20 rule implies the company should eliminate some products and eliminate some low income-producing clients.

80% of the gross profit is made on the youngest used cars in inventory. The focus is getting the highest gross profit and moving the newest units. The stock world says the trend is your friend, which means if the industry is increasing in value, then most of the stocks in the industry will go up in value. If the industry is taking a financial hit, than most of the stocks (including the leaders of the industry) should decrease in price. Motivational speakers call it 'flow' or 'working with the universe.' Use the 80/20 rule and watch your profits skyrocket.

## THE RULE OF FIVE

The Rule of Five is to make a list of the top five things you have to do in a day. Managers forget the simple things. Do this for 30 days and have your employees do it for 30 days as well. The goal is a minimum increase of 30% in efficiency.

## DELEGATE, DELETE AND SAY 'NO'

Figure out your hourly rate and delegate everything below your hourly rate. Most of your day should be delegating. Free up your time to accomplish the tasks which are most important. Delegating can be a challenge. If you are not able to delegate, then you have incompetent people or you have a control issue. Handle the challenges and delegate.

Deleting will make your world happier. You may delete employees, vendors, tasks, etc.; ...the purpose of deleting is to free up your time. Some people delete all of the negative people in their life. Find one person a month to delete.

Knowing what you now know, would you get involved in this relationship or job? The question is zero-based thinking. Knowing what you now know, would you hire this salesperson? If the answer is no, then get out of the situation as fast as you can.

Nancy Reagan said to just say 'no.' Say 'no' more, and say 'yes' little. You should under promise and over deliver. Show up early and achieve more by being focused (saying no and delegating).

## HIGH STANDARDS

Tony Robbins says to have high standards. High standards will make all the difference in the world. The standards should not be perfection. Standards should be volume. Focus on the volume. If the goal is 100 units a month, then make the goal based on 90% of the month. High standards should be based on perfection if you are a pharmacist.

To have high standards, you should find your personal weakness and make your personal weakness one of your strengths. Every discipline affects the rest. You can't call yourself an intellectual and a smoker at the same time. Some people have a weakness with exercise. Go the extra mile in order to achieve your high standards.

A measure of high standards for the car world could be 180 used cars sold in a month. A measure of high standards in the medical field was shipping to 100,000 patients in a month. If you have 'day's sales outstanding' of 10 days, then you have a great standard. Find a standard and make certain the standard is a high standard.

## FIRE. READY. AIM.

Fire; ready; aim means to be first to market and not to spend too much time thinking or planning. After action is taken, you get to correct your work. Take away procrastination. It is about action, which others may call courage. Eventually you will have courage. Speed and not being afraid of failure over time, will yield results.

General Colin Powel said indecision has cost Americans billions more than a wrong decision. Taking action and quickly changing direction in your travel can be a wise move; however, if you are working for a large company, changing your direction or marketing is a slow event. Are you a speedboat or a cruise ship, when it comes to changing your vessel's direction?

Action and speed combined equals results. The results can be profitable or a major error. Over time, 90% of our decisions will turn out to be wrong decisions. Accept that over time, 90% of our decisions will be wrong and it is okay to mess up.

A manager has about half a dozen goals: keep your job, sales, great advertising, employee retention, employee recruiting, great products, happy/loyal customers and the house/company to make a profit. The focus should be on the speed of a sale and employee retention, in my opinion, while being legally compliant. The next focus is on duplication: copy somebody who is successful. Find bottlenecks in the process and eliminate those bottlenecks.

## BEST MANAGERS

The best managers keep an eye on their numbers: sales per hour, time on the phone, sales per day, cost of adverting per sale. The best managers give the producers the house transactions and increase the best salespeople's income. The best managers leave on time, but show up early. The best managers are loyal to the company and to the sales team. The best managers make people laugh.

The best managers will focus on the salesperson's income and not the house's income. When the salesperson has a drop in income, that is when the manager steps in. The salesperson is king. The salespeople are the horses pulling the chariot or company. Treat the horses politely and feed them and reward your team.

The best companies conduct daily, weekly, monthly or quarterly promotions for the salespeople. The best salespeople review the current month and the following month with the manager. Salespeople want the pay plan, the products and customers to sell. Managers want great salespeople. Make them laugh, respect them, pay them well, have constant promotions, and give variety and certainty with work functions, which will increase the fun. Great managers are accountable.

## SUCCESS SECRET RULES

1. Don't Complain and Don't Explain.
2. Be responsible and accountable.
3. Keep your promises.
4. If you cannot keep your promises, let people know quickly.
5. Keep your eyes on the prize. Stay focused.
6. What you focus on comes about.

7. The trend is your friend: follow flow.

8. Have high standards.

9. Follow the 80/20 Rule.

10. Delegate.

11. Delete.

12. Say 'No.'

13. Focus on growth.

14. Focus on Health.

15. Get your sleep.

16. Take action, and courage will follow with results.

17. Shoot for the stars and you will hit the moon.

18. Do the <u>five</u> most important things everyday.

19. Write your goals daily.

20. Adopt an attitude of gratitude: be grateful.

21. Tell the truth.

22. Show up early.

23. Be approachable.

24. The microphone is always on: make sure it can be printed on the front page of the newspaper.

25. Give compliments.

26. Do less to achieve more.

27. Get a mentor/coach.

28. Praise in public; criticize in private.

## QUESTIONS MANAGERS SHOULD ASK

• Is there something you are not telling me that you should be telling me?

• Is there something else you want to tell me?

• Is it true what I'm hearing about you?

• Do you want to ask me something?

- What is reality?

- What is the Reader's Digest version of this story?

- If you did know, what would the answer be?

## RICH DAD'S ADVICE

Depending on your industry, it can be easier to replace a customer than to replace a salesperson. The sales manager needs to keep both the customers and the sales staff happy. How long does it take to replace a good salesperson and how long does it take to replace a customer. The acquisition cost of a new client in the medical field was about $50-$350. The training cost was much greater in the medical industry. The salesperson wins (compared to the client). The cost of acquiring a new car transaction was about $250. The focus is on making and keeping the sales team happy. If the acquisition cost for a new customer was much higher, then focus would be on the client.

The customer is always right. Sometimes, the customer will be upset and want something. "What do you think is fair?" The client will usually ask for less. "If you were in my shoes, what would you do?" The customer will give you an answer, which is usually less painful or less costly, than your suggestion or solution. People will always be unhappy. When you solve the challenge, say, "Now that settles that, doesn't it?" If there is still an issue, then the customer will let you know. Finally say, "Oh, by the way," which will change gear or shift gears or change the subject.

My Rich Dad said if he ever over-ruled a manager by taking the advice of the sales person (over the manager), then he would have to fire the manager (because the manager didn't have as much respect). So my Rich Dad would usually let the poor ideas of a manager continue, unless the manager's days were numbered.

My Rich Dad told me that average sales people can become great managers. Great managers will usually make less money than the top sales people. Top sales people can have a job for a decade while the manager's position can have turnover. The money may not be in management. The money is in sales and being a business owner. The stress is in management. The reason you stay a manager is because you cannot sell, but you can manage. Those who cannot sell either manage or train or get out of the selling profession. Management is not about a title. Management can be about the training you need to become a business owner. Management in Corporate America can become a career.

My Rich Dad said to always have a backup plan, and a backup plan for the backup plan. Know your options and find more ways to succeed if your plan does not work. What would happen if your assumptions were wrong? My Rich Dad succeeded partially because of having more options or plans to succeed. Managers need routine and more backup plans.

Zig Ziglar said if it is not right at home, then it will not be right at work. Zig said when you are at work, you are thinking about home and when you are at home you are thinking about work. Zig believes in building values, which build a company. By building the person, the company will have less work to do to build a company.

Follow the money and you will find you don't make your money the way you think you make your money. By following the money you will find answers.

The man is the head of the family, but the woman is the neck. The neck controls the head. The woman is usually correct. If husbands follow this advice, then they would be happier. If salespeople follow this advice, then their sales would increase.

One of your functions is to get your people to like you, trust you and want to listen to you. In addition, managers need rapport to have their employees come and talk to them. Imagine that in the 80's, the US military took a hit in the dining room/cafeteria, in which a large number of the U.S. servicemen died. The phone rings back in the U.S. and a father answers the phone. He is silent and said he would come (to pick up his son's body at the air force base when the plane landed). The father breaks down and tells his family. A wake is set up. The father has to drive about an hour to where the US carrier unloads caskets. Each casket has a US flag on it. Then a young military man comes off the plane. It is his son. The father falls to his knees and cries and then the living son (who was supposed to be in the casket) breaks down crying, too. The father cannot talk, as he sees his son alive. The father doesn't know his son was smoking, and was not in the cafeteria when everybody died (in his son's troop). The father won't let his son go. The two of them go to the wake to end all wakes at the family home. This is the kind of story which a manager hears only if the employee trusts the manager. Establish trust with honesty and caring.

When your people are willing to tell you about their personal life, they are also willing to tell you about the business, which will assist you. Tom Hopkins said, "Never take advice from somebody more messed up than you are." So take advice from your top producers. The feedback will keep you on course. The producers will try to manipulate you as well.

My Rich Dad's last bit of advice to me was to stop focusing on the millions of dollars and to enjoy each day. Tom Hopkins states there are 86,400 seconds in each day. The phrases 'I love you, I am so grateful to be with you and thank you for being with me' started flowing out of me. My Rich Dad died with cancer. He knew over a decade in advance of his condition. Every day he gave to his wife. Most days were fun. He made the 86,400 seconds count. My Rich Dad also taught me well. If you don't get it right at home, then you probably won't get it right at work. When the home life flows and the work life is taking off, then the money comes.

## MY ADVICE TO MANAGERS

1. Find the top six things you need to master
2. Practice the Rule of Five each day
3. Delegate and learn to say no
4. Practice the 80/20 Rule
5. Give credit to everybody
6. Be polite
7. Achieve more at work so you can achieve everything away from work
8. Work harder on yourself than you do on your job
9. What you focus on comes about
10. Have three backup plans
11. Know your numbers
12. Do less (tasks) so you can accomplish more (tasks -- which equals real or greater results)

My advice is complicated. First, there are half-a-dozen things you need to master. Find those half-a-dozen things. Second, write down the five most important things you need to accomplish every day. Third, Delegate more; delete activities and say 'no' more often. Fourth, focus on the 20% activities, which will yield you 80% of your results. Fifth, give the credit to others and be polite. Sixth, focus more on yourself than you do on your job. Become the person whom you need to be – in order to achieve more. Achieve all this with high goals, which will force you to change.

Live as an example to others and live for your life outside of work.

## About John

John Jochem is a bestselling author. He has co-authored books with Jack Canfield of *Chicken Soup for the Soul,* Tom Hopkins, who wrote *How to Master the Art of Selling,* and Brian Tracy, who wrote *Goals.* John's books are *The Success Secret, In It To Win It* and *Counter Attack.* John is a certified Zig Ziglar speaker and trainer, a success coach and a consultant. John has spent months on the road with Tony Robbins, and has been mentored by Jack Canfield and Brian Tracy. In 2000, Tom Hopkins named John #1 out of a hundred thousand students that he trained. Corporately, John worked for 5 of the top 10 Diabetic Supply companies, and his best month in sales was 1,250 individual transactions. John did corporate acquisition for three of the top four Diabetic Supply companies; the biggest was about $25,000,000. His largest advertising budget was $62,000,000. He has worked with the #2 power wheelchair company and helped to establish the #2 respiratory wholesale company in America.

Educationally, John's highest level is doctorate work. He has an MBA from the University of Phoenix and an undergraduate BBA with dual majors in Marketing and Finance from the University of Miami. He has taught college students business concepts in management courses.

To contact John for consulting or coaching, email him at: johnfjochem@gmail.com .

CHAPTER 14

# Shining the Brass When Building Leaders

## By Azhar Khan

Growing up as a little boy, I was very curious. I would pull apart my toys to see exactly how they worked. I was always told that I was far too young to be reading the type of books that I surrounded myself with. Sometimes these books made sense and when they did not, I would nevertheless still see the words on paper and tried to memorize them as best as I could.

My master plan at the age of 10 was to consume as much information as possible that could help others in the future. My mind categorized and referenced words and sentences like a computer does. My imagination grew every day from discoveries I made. It literally catapulted my mind and urged me to explore and see the world.

One day, my late mother called me to come and learn how to shine the large brass vase and tray ornaments that she kept in the lounge. Just imagine how disgruntled I felt at the thought of having to waste my valuable time and do something as mundane as this!

The hand-beaten scalloped-edged tray measured two feet in circumference. The vase, like the tray, had also been handcrafted with delicate grand old world charm, and matched the tray perfectly. Mother constantly made a point of telling my siblings and I that it was not actually a set, just a coincidence.

She had inherited it from her mother who had bought them separately from two different places. Both the tray and vase were placed on top of a large white crocheted table doily, which was draped over the coffee table. I always remember how uncanny it was, that the two when brought together looked like a set and fitted so perfectly together.

Cleaning and polishing the brass I thought, how ridiculous! I had so many other more important things to do and think about. This was hardly going to be stimulating for me, and certainly not something that I wanted to be involved with. What was mother thinking, I thought? After all, there is staff to do this work, I muttered to myself.

I grew up in Zimbabwe where it was, and still is, common to employ domestic household staff. Cleaning and polishing the brassware was one of the chores ordinarily done by them. In most cases, the staff would be responsible for the general running of the household. My parents ensured that I got a rich and diverse upbringing for which I will always be truly grateful. One of the valuable lessons that I learnt from constantly having staff around me was "people management." So when mother asked me to come and polish the brass, I raised my eyebrows.

"Why should I do it?" I boldly and bluntly asked my mother. "Tell Rena to do it, after all, that is her job." I said. My Mother shook her head, and with tears in her eyes said, "I did not ask Rena, because … I'm asking you. If I could do it myself, I would do it, but I can't hold the tray or the vase for long and it needs to be cleaned properly. I want you, my son, to learn and understand the sentimental value that I have for the tray and vase.

"Did you know that they belonged to my mother; your grand mother, so keeping it looking clean and shining means a lot to me. One day you'll understand," she said. Her big brown eyes looked so hurt at the thought that I did not want to do something for her that they welled up with disappointment. Never wanting her to ever feel this way about me, my heart melted and I felt really selfish for not realizing how much this brass tray and vase meant to her. I immediately picked up the polish and cloth and an old newspaper to start cleaning. I'd seen Rena do it several times so this was not going to take long and it would make her happy. "Let's just get it done." I mumbled to myself again.

My thoughts were already planning the rest of my day. I always had something better to do, so I thought. Often the biggest learning's in life are not "in your face" for you to choose. The biggest learning's I've had in life were hidden in the little things. I'm sure you've all heard the saying "take time to appreciate the small things in life."

I was about 9 years old when my mother was involved in a car crash that disabled her from the neck down. The best neuro-surgeons in the world said that she would never walk again. She proved them all wrong. With the right attitude and positive mindset, mother took just over 6 years to teach herself to walk again. Against all odds she did.

This was the reason why she could not clean the brass herself. She still did not have feeling in her left hand, so holding a big brass tray and vase was going to be just too much for her. Having a disability was not going to stop her. She still had her eyes, and they could see if something was right or wrong. Mother knew that if she really wanted it done well, she would have to show someone how to shine it the way her mother had taught her, in exactly the same way, so that it would always look at it's best. She had asked me because she wanted to pass on something that meant so much to her.

And so I began to shine the brass. I took the cloth and poured on the polish specifically made for shining brass items, that I had seen Rena using. My mother watched as I franticly rubbed the polish on. I rubbed and buffed and the more I polished the worse the brass looked. As I rubbed in the liquid polish, it started turning black, so I stopped. In some places the polish started to instantly dry and as it dried, my worst nightmare began unfolding before my eyes and the feeling of despair came over me. This did not look right. I knew this was not supposed to happen. What have I done, I thought. Brass is not meant to turn white? It was like someone had spilt cream all over the tray as the polish continued to dry.

It was then that I realised that this was not going to be an "easy chore," and would take a lot longer than I had first hoped for. At this point, the tray looked worse than before I had started it. I thought I would just cover all the brass with more polish and once I had spread every last drop all over, I would take a cloth and shine it. After all that's what it said on the bottle and so that's obviously what I should do. The quicker I can complete this, the sooner I will be able to go and watch TV.

Never having shined brass before, I of course was unaware of the many pitfalls that could be encountered along the way!

The moment the polish dries, you have to spend even more time and apply extra effort to get it clean again. In addition, as you apply more and more of the polish, it dries up and leaves a thin hard film on the surface. This dried polish now needs to be chipped away and leaves a dull residue. There is now also a great chance that you may scratch the brass.

And then there is another problem, which I think is even worse! If the polish is still wet and you rub too hard, the polishing becomes a bigger task, as the polish actually turns from an opaque cream into a black colour that leaves black streaks all over the area that you are polishing.

So now it takes even longer and requires a lot more rubbing, until you are finally exhausted from all the rubbing and shining, whilst at this stage you feel as if you haven't even started! By the time you figure this out the brass looks dull, definitely cleaner, but has totally lost its brilliance and has black streaks in some places or has a dark film on it. When you begin going over the areas that you had previously tried to shine, the process tends to repeat itself.

You also need to be aware not to let the cloth that you are using touch any of the completed polished areas, as should this happen, then the cleaned area will again have black marks left from the cloth........... back to square one, more polishing needed! It is at this point when you feel that you are in a loop with no way out. Seeing my frustration mother smiled at me and said. "Not as easy as it looks?"

"No!" I exclaimed " I'm exhausted and I have been here for over half an hour already. I feel as though I haven't even started yet." Mother laughed when she saw what I'd done. "There is no easy way to shine the brass, but there are ways to make it easier," she said. "First, don't try to do it all at once. Try a little bit at a time, and you will find it easier to manage," she said. With that she picked up the polish cloth with her one good hand and showed me the strategy handed down to her by her mother. "Here's what you need to do."

"Take the cloth and put a little polish on it. Then rub a small area until you see it turn black like this." She said. "Then immediately when it turns black, shine it with a piece of newspaper. You won't get a better shine if you tried with any other purpose-made shining cloth on the market. The more often you do it, the better your brass will shine. Just old newspaper and quickly wipe off the black polish and it will begin to shine quite rapidly. It's a secret technique that my mother taught me and now I'm passing it on to you, my son." She smiled with pride. I will always remember that moment sitting with her in the kitchen at the table. That day I learnt some valuable lessons about life and the path that some of us choose.

I decided to use the brass lesson at one of my seminars to gauge the re-action of the attendees. I brought the large brass tray and vase ornament and laid out a selection of various polishes. I then proceeded to ask the attendees to go about shining the brass. Then I watched their reaction in attempting this task.

They formed small committees to find the best way. Some people at-tempted to try, whilst others stood by and watched. My conditions were clear. Everyone must have a go. But some gave up when they saw oth-ers struggling. Some even tried short cuts, and attempted to use other polishes that I had made available in the room. Those that tried did not get very far and became disillusioned when they saw that others were failing. Several people "Googled" and "YouTubed" in an attempt to find to an online solution. Others wondered if there could possibly be an APP for this. No one could agree on a strategy. No one delivered results.

After watching the attendees actions, I gave a demonstration and sur-prised everyone when I showed them how this, my childhood learn-ing's, could be applied to business:

- Your curiosity should have no boundaries; experiment and curi-ous about everything in life.

- Just like the vase and tray came together from different parts of the world, they still made a great partnership. Imagine the way you bring things together and master the art of complementary association.

- Never assume anything. You can choose to be a bystander and expect others around you to complete tasks. Or you can join in and discover its fun to be a part of results.

- The smallest jobs have meaning and direction when you choose to see how best it serves you.

- You can only learn from your mistakes, but you have to take action first or fear will prevent you overcoming the obstacles in your path.

- The time that you spend on others is a blessing. Try to never take the small things for granted. They are what make big things bigger.

- Be open and aware of opportunity, you never know when someone is about to profoundly change your life by an "easy chore."

In completing the chore at home, I spent the next hour cleaning the brass on the table in the kitchen and chatting with mother. What I learnt that day became a metaphor for almost everything in my life, and now forms the basis of the principles that I use when mentoring and coaching leadership in business.

1. Discover the unique technique that will differentiate your business, product, or individual. Then ensure that you are spending time on nurturing that part so that it grows stronger. Just like shining one small part of the brass at a time.

2. Promote your ability to your market, workplace, or territory continuously and frequently. The more you shine the brighter you look.

3. Serve others without spreading yourself thin or it's going to take a lot of burning the midnight oil and tons of unnecessary hard work to make your brass shine. If you don't, you may never succeed in achieving anything substantial without exhausting yourself, especially if you aren't prepared adequately.

4. Do what you love and devote yourself to what you do, because you will have to work at it from all angles, and for it to shine the way you want it.

5. Work and play with people you love to be with. Life's too short to shine anything, any other way. Spend time everyday with anyone who fills your life with joy and happiness.

6. Don't ever see your contribution as wasted, mundane or boring no matter how small or minimised it may seem. Whatever you do, always give it your best shot. Start with the resources you have today, that you can build on. Shine them bright for all to see and you will attract to you others that shine just as bright.

I now know that I could chose to see shining the brass as a chore, or it can be a way to spend precious time with mother. Today I know the value of shining the brass at a corporate level. It was a turning point in my life. The value of my mother delegating that chore to me left a huge impact on my life. Slowly, every detail of the event filtered through and every time I tell this story, I gain further insight into its deeper resolution. You just can never prepare for moments like this. When they happen they remain with you forever. What would you choose? Wouldn't you agree that it's how you look at anything that really matters in the grand scheme of things?

Remember to Share your Brilliance. Shine Bright.

## About Azhar

Name:     Azhar Khan
City:       Gold Coast
Company: Sabistar Pty Ltd
Website:  www.azharkhan.me

Azhar is a solutions and media architect, international speaker, consultant, mentor and coach, with diverse experience in many industry sectors. For over 20 years he has built a valuable repertoire of knowledge that combines with his technical skillset and competencies for training and leadership development.

Born in Zimbabwe, Africa in 1971, he began his own publishing company at the age of 24, which later developed into an advertising agency that worked with blue chip corporate companies and developing communities in 3$^{rd}$ world countries. He continues to create solutions for businesses and non-governmental organisations.

His strength lies in understanding business on a global scale, combined with creative, technical and production skills. He seamlessly integrates customer journeys with highly enriched user experiences to build vision and purpose to any project. He understands the complexity of technology along with global business and simplifies the jargon in a way that leads to the successful execution of strategies, tactics and business plans.

Azhar moved to Australia in 2001 and spent over 10 years researching personal development, NLP and achievement technologies, discovering how they influence mass communication. During this time, he extended his entrepreneurial skills to magazine publishing and web development in the tourism industry. In 2006/7 he spent time in Dubai discovering global focus areas for consumers and how new modern global cultural centers will influence global change in the future.

His dedication to technology and its uses has enabled him to present, and work with, Fortune 500 companies, governments and individuals around the globe.

Azhar is also a Certified Master Practitioner in Neuro Linguistic Programming and Neurological Re-patterning. He is a Demartini Method ™ Facilitator for Groups and and is a Certified Performance and Results Coach.

Website contact: http://www.azharkhan.me

# CHAPTER 15

# Revitalize Your Sales Force Strategy In 90 Days

## By Steve Maughan

If you've recently taken charge of a sales team and you're not sure where to begin, then this chapter is for you. Or maybe your sales team lacks the drive and sense of urgency that will be required to meet the corporate objectives. Either way, this chapter is for you.

If you follow the plan and address the highlighted areas you **will** increase the business success of your sales force. I have personally implemented these approaches for companies large and small in over forty countries around the world. On my travels, I found the key to a successful sales force strategy is not trying to accomplish 101 projects or initiatives, it's focusing on the core fundamentals that are set out in this chapter.

Let's start with the foundations for all sales force planning - the customer segmentation...

### STEP 1 - CUSTOMER SEGMENTATION

The key principle underlying all customer segmentation work is:

*Not All Customers Are the Same*

Some customers have more sales potential, while others have less. If we can find out which customers are more likely to respond to our selling effort then we can focus our effort on these customers and increase the sales productivity.

The most basic mistake companies make when segmenting customers is to base the segmentation criteria solely on your own sales. This is a *tail-chasing* strategy which drives activity, but doesn't move you towards the goal of increasing sales and growing the business. Effectively, sales reps who follow this strategy are account managers and not *rainmaking* salesmen. To correct this problem you must shift the focus toward **potential sales**. For example, if your team calls on General Practitioners, you could focus on the number of doctors in the practice to drive selling activity. The key is to select a measure (or proxy) for sales potential which is:

- Highly correlated to actual sales potential
- Visible (so anyone can measure or verify it)
- Simple (so everyone can understand it)

The process of defining each segment should be carried out in conjunction with an analysis of coverage and call-frequency planning. For this you must define the following:

- **Coverage** - the proportion of each segment which will receive any calls at all
- **Frequency** - for those whom are called on, the average number of annual calls they will receive

From this you can calculate the planned calls using the simple formula:

*Planned Calls = Segment Size x Coverage (%) x Call Frequency*

Use this formula to balance the Planned Calls with the Call Capacity of the sales team.

When you are reviewing a proposed Customer Segmentation scheme, always evaluate it against the following criteria:

- Is there enough differentiation in effort between the high potential and low potential segments?
- Is there too much selling effort going against one segment? For example, if there are three segments A, B and C - with A receiv-

ing 40 calls each per year and B receiving 6 calls each per year, it is likely that the 40th call to the A customers can be better utilized by increasing the coverage or frequency to B customers.

- Is one segment too big? For example, if you have three segments A, B and C - and segment B accounts for 90% of all customers then you should probably re-segment to even-out the segment sizes.

Customer Segmentation is the foundation of virtually all sales force analytics and optimization. It's worth investing the time and resources to get it right. And based on our experience, once you do get it right you can expect sales to increase anywhere from +3% to +30% over three years. Of course this depends upon the initial condition of the customer segmentation.

## STEP 2 - SALES FORCE SIZE AND RESOURCE ALLOCATION

Once you have a solid Customer Segmentation in place, it's time to move on and look at how much sales force resource you need; and how you're going to structure the sales force.

### Size Matters

The sales force headcount is an important question for two reasons. Firstly, sales reps are expensive; a typical professional sales rep in the US cost between $140k and $300k. So if you have too many reps you'll be wasting a lot of money. And secondly, sales reps are a potent driver of sales - often the key link between a company and its customers. If you don't have enough reps you'll be leaving profitable sales dollars on the table (which your competition will be happy to pick up).

So how do you determine the sales force size?

The number one mistake companies make when deciding on the size of their sales force is to base the decision on the ratio of *sales-per-rep*. Companies who fall into this trap will add reps when, and only when, the sales-per-rep ratio hits a certain level. More worryingly, they will reduce the headcount when the ratio falls to a certain level.

This is bad for a number of reasons:

1. Philosophically, the sales reps should be driving the sales, and not the sales determining the number of reps, i.e., it's a reversal of the true cause-and-effect relationship

2. There is no "correct" ratio

3. The ratio can _always_ be improved by reducing the size of the sales force

4. The approach doesn't take into consideration the needs of the customers, the needs of the products or the competitive environment

A much better approach is _sales response function analysis._ In its most basic form, each product is analyzed separately to determine the upside potential and downside risks. This is normally done by analyzing:

- Level of coverage of key customers
- Frequency of calling on key customers
- Competitive environment
- Product benefits
- Momentum of product sales
- Historical performance

This is not an exhaustive list of factors but it includes the most important ones. From these factors, each product's sales response function is created. This is normally an annual view of the cause-and-effect relationship between the level of sales resource and sales. The diagram below is an example of a sales response function for a fictional product:

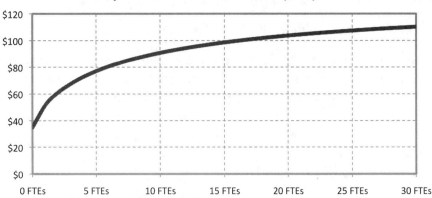

Conceptually once you understand this relationship for each product you can do two things:

1. You can *optimize* the allocation of selling effort across the portfolio to maximize the overall long-term profitability of the business.

2. You can assess the financial impact of adding to, or taking from, the size of the sales force.

This approach has added billions of dollars of incremental sales and profitability for large multinationals. It was popularized during the eighties and nineties by large consulting companies who developed their own software and processes to implement response function analysis for their clients.

Response function analytics does require specialized optimization software. This is the only real downside of this methodology. Until recently this type of software was a challenge to develop. However, if you visit **http://www.cozmix.com/in-it-to-win-it/** you can find out about Size-Mix, a new cost-effective solution that you can easily use to implement response function analytics for your sales force.

## STEP 3 - SALES TERRITORY DESIGN

Once you know the ideal size, structure and focus for your sales team you must dig a little deeper and implement these plans at the territory level. This means you must create a new sales territory design, which reflects the new sales force size and focus. For many sales forces, the sales territory alignment is an often-overlooked source of productivity enhancement. But there is no reason why this should be the case for you. Here's a high level view of the process I recommend.

Sales Territory Design Process

The sales territory alignment is often the silent killer of sales force productivity. At the feet-on-the-street level, the reps are rarely in a position to evaluate how good or bad their territory really is compared to neighboring territories. While at the management level it is usually assumed that the territories are reasonably good. Yet analysis by Northwestern University has shown that implementing a good sales territory re-alignment can deliver an incremental uplift of up to 15% in sales, over three years.

So here's the process we recommend you follow to improve your sales territories:

**(a). Decide On the Fundamental Building Blocks of the Alignment:**
Most sales forces are built around postcodes or zip codes. Some are built around counties or other administrative boundaries. The key is to build around the boundaries which make sense for your customers and your business.

**(b). Define What an Ideal Territory Looks Like:**
At this stage you should focus on the numeric measure. Ideally the data you collect should have at least two components. There must be a proxy for workload (i.e., actual time required to service each zip code or postcode) and a proxy for sales potential. Hopefully the data for both workload and sales potential have already been collected as part of the customer segmentation analysis

**(c). Assess the Current Sales Territory Alignment:**
Use the data to assess the quality of the current alignment. Look at the variation in workload and sales potential across the whole sales force. How many territories are within ±15% of the average workload and sales potential? If there are more than 30% of the territories outside the ±15% of the average workload and potential then you really need to consider a full re-alignment and move on to step 4. If there are less than 30% of territories outside of our target range then you can maintain the stability of the alignment and plan to re-audit the alignment next year.

**(d). Redesign the Territories**
Load the data into a Geographic Information Systems such as AlignMix (www.alignmix.com), which is a specialized sales territory design solution. Make changes to the alignment and use the reporting tools to assess the alignment balance.

Once you have a preliminary re-alignment you must involve the first line managers. Give them the opportunity to adjust the alignment within a certain range. This will provide the opportunity for them to add their local knowledge about customers and geography. It will also give them some *skin-in-the-game* when they are selling the new alignment to their reps!

## STEP 4 - DEFINE THE BONUS PLAN

Once you've got to this point you have the high level strategy. You know the size, structure and focus for the sales force; and you know how it will be implemented at the territory level. Now you need to motivate the sales force to follow the plan - that's where the bonus plan comes in.

Getting the bonus plan right is a tough task and a full discussion of the issues is well outside the scope for this chapter. What I can give you are three questions to ask when presented with a bonus plan. These are intended to cut to the heart of the matter and highlight the most common weaknesses in a bonus plan.

### (i). Is "Total Sales" the only measure of Success?

Bonus plans often focus too much on total sales. This is a problem for a number of reasons. Firstly, the sales generated this year are a result of more than just this year's selling effort. They are the result of many years of brand and relationship building. So to bonus only on total sales is to compensate a sales reps for this year's *and previous year's* selling effort. The problem is normally more evident when there are small territories which are growing quickly. These territories are penalized compared with the *fat cat* territories, which have been built up over years, but where the sales reps do little other than *socialize* with their "mates."

Secondly, by focusing on total sales there is no incentive for the reps to manage their portfolio of product. For example, some products may have higher margins; yet to the reps, every dollar in sales is the same as every other dollar. This also makes launching new products more difficult, as the reps are will most likely be reluctant to invest the time to promote a product with low sales at the expense of the larger products in the portfolio.

### (ii). Does the Plan incentivize the reps to keep their foot on the pedal all year?

With sales-quota based plans there can be tendency for the reps to stop selling (or at least slow down) towards the end of the year. This can happen for two reasons. If the rep has made their quota, they don't want to grow the business any further as this will only increase their quota for next year. On the other hand, if the rep isn't going to reach their quota they can stop selling for the same reason - they want a lower quota next year.

### (iii). Does the Plan incentivize the rep to follow the corporate strategy?

This is really the key question. A plan should be structured such that everyone is motivated to follow the corporate strategy. This means they should be rewarded for selling the right products to the right customers at the right price.

## LIKELY SALES UPLIFT AND TIMETABLE

The sales uplift which you achieve as a result of focusing on these four core topics will vary depending upon your current level of sophistication and the amount of change in your business. The table below shows the range of three-year sales increases that I've seen. I've also listed a guide as to the time required to address each topic.

| Lever of Sales Productivity | Likely Improvement in Sales (over 3 years) | Time Required to Implement |
|---|---|---|
| Customer Segmentation | 3% - 35% | 4 Weeks |
| Sizing & Resource Allocation | 3% - 30% | 3 Weeks |
| Territory Design | 5% - 15% | 2 Weeks |
| Bonus Plan | 0% - 40% | 3 Weeks |

## SUMMARY

The topics covered are the foundations for all successful sales forces. These are the fundamentals, but due to limited space I haven't been able to cover everything in this chapter. So if you're serious about improving your sales force productivity, I've put together some free resources that I'd like to send you. You'll find more details at: http://www.cozmix.com/in-it-to-win-it/

First, there is a series of sales force strategy tutorial videos. This is three full hours of high quality sales force strategy training. These were initially commissioned for $10k but as a reader of *In It To Win It,* they are yours for free.

Secondly, there are three more in-depth reports that I'd like to send you:

- *Six Ways to Optimize Your Sales Force Size*
- *Five Questions to Ask Before You Design Your Sales Territories*
- *Ten Pitfalls of Sales Force Planning (...and How to Avoid Them)*

To access these additional resources, go to: **http://www.cozmix.com/ in-it-to-win-it/** and sign up now.

If you have any sales force strategy questions, you can email me at **steve.maughan@cozmix.com** and I'll be happy to address them.

## About Steve

Steve has spent the last twenty-two years helping companies improve their sales force strategy. He has managed sales force strategy projects in over forty countries worldwide. Steve started his career at ZS Associates and has also been a Partner with Accenture. Currently Steve is President of Cozmix Inc. based in Florida.

Steve holds two Masters degrees in Engineering from Cambridge University. When he is not delving into sales force strategy issues, he has a quirky hobby as he likes to relax by programming chess computers.

Steve lives in Florida with his beautiful wife Stephanie and their two wonderful daughters, Evie and Pippa.

# CHAPTER 16

# Building Your "Why"

## By David Hull

### WAIT, WAIT, WAIT!!!

***Don't skip this chapter*** just because you're telling yourself, "Oh here's the fluff part. I want the meat and potatoes for my business. I don't need some so-called 'motivational, inspiring nonsense.'"

My friend, if you're one of the few people who think this way, then let me set you straight right now. There's absolutely nothing more important for the success of your business than to know clearly *why* you're doing this business.

*"Okay, okay then, you want my "WHY?" It's the same thing EVERYONE wants... MONEY! There, I've told you my "WHY." So NOW I can skip this chapter?"*

NOPE... No one does a business, any business in fact, just to *"make money."* It's not the "money" that people want; it's what that money will *do* for individuals. And money does something different for everyone. And *that,* my friend, is what we need to have you *clearly understand and articulate to yourself.*

## WHAT WOULD HAVING MORE MONEY
## MEAN FOR YOU?

You see, at some point you *will* want to quit your business, *that* I can assure you. Whether it's a Pool Route, a Cleaning Business, a Franchise or a Network Marketing business, at some point you will want to quit. I've owned several businesses over the years (including Network Marketing) and wanted to quit them *all* at one time or another. Like any business, you're going to have your good days and your bad days. In particular with Network Marketing, because there's not a large investment of money involved in getting it started, so it's really easy to walk away. And sad to say, so many people do, giving up on their dreams of a secure and lasting financial future. It's because of that, you have to have a rock solid anchor to hold on to and be able to weather through the tough times, so you can enjoy the incredibly *wonderful* times that owning your own business can afford you!

In a word? You need a *really strong...* **WHY?**

### A POWERFUL STORY OF WHY

One of the best stories I ever heard in connection with developing a strong "why" was told to me about 14 years ago by a Doctor trying to help me lose weight. He asked me "why" I wanted to lose weight.

I told him, *"Well, to look better and feel better, of course."*

*"No, David... really... WHY do you want to lose weight? Because I assure you I'm going to give you a diet and exercise plan that, at some point, you WILL want to quit on. You're excited about it now, but at some point during this process that excitement will wane and you're going to want to quit and go back to the way it was before. So you need to tell me the REAL reason you want to lose that weight."*

While I was sitting there trying to come up with a clever answer that would impress him, he proceeded to tell me a story about New York's World Trade Centers. (Keep in mind, this was 14 years ago, long before the tragedy of 9/11.) He asked me:

*"David, did you know that the Twin Towers of the World Trade Center are 110 stories high and, at their closest point, are only 200 feet apart from each other? Now let me ask you; if I were to have a steel I-beam, one foot*

*thick, securely bolted down between the two buildings, would you walk across it if I dared you?"*

I remember thinking to myself, *"I'm PAYING this guy?"* I was beginning to doubt the sanity of my Doctor and that's always a cause for concern. So I answered him as best I could. *"No Doc, only an insane person would do that."*

*"I'm glad you said that David, so now we know that you are in fact sane. But then let me ask you this: would you walk across that beam for 10 Million Dollars? Think about it before you answer. What if a man was standing on the other side of that beam, and in his hand he held a bag of cash worth 10 Million Dollars. Would you cross it then?"*

Well now, wait a second. Ten *Million* Dollars? That kind of money would be life changing. It would change *everything* for not only me, but for my family and my friends too. I could do a *lot* of good in life with that kind of money. So I thought about it and before I answered him, I imagined how I could accomplish this seemingly impossible feat.

I envisioned myself lying on my stomach, flat across the beam, arms and legs clamped around it like a baby chimpanzee clamps onto his mother as she swings from vine to vine, a grip so fiercely tight that only God himself could pry me from it. I could see myself crawling across the expanse like an inchworm, inch-by-precious-inch. Butt up, butt down, butt up, butt down… It could take me all day for all I care. But I could do it! For 10 MILLION Dollars… are you kidding me? I COULD DO IT!

*"Yes Doc! Absolutely I would do it for 10 MILLION Dollars! When can we go??!"*

*"Wow, that's great David… Oh… but wait. I forgot to tell you, there are some conditions on that beam that you need to know about."*

Yeah, I knew it! That's just the way life is, always "something" that keeps us from getting what we really want. *"Okay Doc, what's the catch?"*

And as if he had been reading my thoughts, he said; *"Well you see David, you're not allowed to just lay on the beam. You can't just crawl across it. You'll need to stand and simply walk across it."*

Ah, Shoot! You see, now he had me thinking about that 10 Million Dollars. I was already spending it; my kids were going to the finest schools and in the best neighborhoods. My Mom was living in her new home, complete with maids and butlers, and she was telling all her friends what a wonderful son she had. My wife and I were traveling the world and enjoying life like we never thought possible. We were helping people all over. And now I have to *stand???* But… it *IS* 12 inches wide. And if I keep *focused* and *not* look down… perhaps…

With quite a bit less enthusiasm, I answered him: *"Well Doc… umm… yeah… sure… I think I might still do it. After all, I mean… 10 Million Dollars WOULD change a LOT in my life."*

"Oh, I forgot David. (Yep, here it comes…) *Those towers were built to withstand large earthquakes so they tend to sway and can move a little on the top floors. More than likely, you'll be feeling a little movement on that beam.* (Ah, heck) *Oh, and I also forgot to mention that it's quite windy up there. And while you're traversing that 200-foot beam, occasionally you can experience gusts of wind up to 60 miles an hour."*

I kind of just stared… 10 MILLION Dollars… *"Ummm…"*

*"You know, David, I think some other people might try it as well. I always imagine that guy taking those first steps."*

*"I see this guy looking across the beam to the other side. I see him longingly staring at that man over there, holding the bag with HIS 10 MILLION Dollars in it. I can just hear the man's thoughts as he's contemplating his first step onto the beam. 'It's only 200 feet across. At two feet a step, that's just 100 steps across. That guy has 10 MILLION DOLLARS in his hand and it's MINE! NOTHING… can stop me!'"*

*"I see him taking his very first step onto the beam, all the confidence in the world on his face and a determination that nothing in the world will be able to stop… 'Just 99 steps more and I'll be rich beyond my wildest dreams.' With such conviction and an enormous smile that looks etched in stone across his face, he moves forward.*

*"I see him taking his second step and glancing up at the man with the bag of 10 MILLION Dollars on the other side, waiting for him to simply arrive and take it, saying to himself: 'Just 98 steps more and never again will I have to listen to a boss tell ME what to do. I'll be my own*

*man!' The enormous smile he was wearing actually gets just a little bigger. And he moves forward."*

*"I see him clearly, as he determinedly takes his 3rd step, concentrating now on the task at hand, all the while locked solidly on his "WHY" he is doing it... 10 MILLION DOLLARS. 'Just 97 steps to go and I'll be admired, loved by all, respected, awed. I'll be the 10-Million-Dollar Man who conquered all fear and walked across the beam between two...' and then the first gust of wind comes by. Not a big one, just enough to..."*

*"The smile vanishes..."*

*"Trying desperately to catch his balance, he flails his arms. Like a circus clown, he dangles one leg out trying to catch his balance. He looks like a man in a comedy scene of an old black and white silent film. For 3, 4, 5 of the longest seconds of his life he prays to God in heaven and makes every promise ever devised by man facing sure extinction, that he would surely fulfill, if God will just keep him from falling."*

*"And as his balance returns to him, he quickly thanks God and at the same time realizes he... is... frozen."*

*Then Doc asked me, "David... do you think that man is thinking about the 96 remaining steps in front of him? Do you think he's thinking about the 10 MILLION Dollars that the man is holding on the other side? Do you think he's still thinking of all he can do with that money, his kid's future, his wife's happiness, the admiration and respect he'll receive from everyone? Or David, wouldn't you agree that that man is laser-focused on just one thing, 'how can I get BACK the 3 steps behind me and LIVE?!!' Can you see him as he's trying to figure out how he can safely turn and not slip in the puddle of "moisture" that has strangely... and suddenly developed at the base of the beam directly below his feet, just after that first gust of wind hit?"*

Yeah I can see that.

But then the Doctor asked me a question that drove the point home to me like nothing could have, and I have never forgotten the feeling I had when he said:

*"So David, let's change something here. I know you have 5-year-old twins, a boy and a girl, right? What are their names again?"*

*"Nicholas and Amanda,"* I replied with suspicion.

*"That's right. So Dave, let me ask you this: what if that man on the other side of the beam was no longer holding a bag of money, but instead was holding little Amanda in his outstretched hands and said to you, 'Come get her... or I'll drop her'?"*

I remember the feeling of the blood draining from my face. The chills that went down my spine and the small hairs that stood up on the back of my neck. I could imagine my beautiful little angel, Amanda, dangling from the man's hand and the intense fear and the tears streaming down on my baby's face. I could see her as she stared across the expanse, and with just one word on her tiny frightened lips, *"Daddy!"*

There was no need for an answer and he could see it. He *knew* that I would, like any parent would, man *or* woman, **RUN** across that beam, without a second thought of the height, the movement, the wind, nothing! I'd be across in about 8 seconds, grab my daughter and *destroy* that man!

The Doctor could see all of that in my face and asked me simply, *"David... What changed?"*

The answer was obvious... my "WHY." What I wouldn't do for **10 MILLION Dollars**, I would do to save something more precious to me than my own life... my little girl.

The Doctor then told me, *"David, your 'WHYs' in life have to be THAT strong if you're ever going to reach your goals."*

You know, my dear friend... *your* "WHY" needs to be *that* strong. *Why* are you *really* doing this business? Whether it's an extra $500/month or $50,000/month... what will that money do for you, for your husband/wife, for your family, for your close friends? What good in the world can you bring about on a bigger scale if you just had a little more money to do it with *and* the freedom of *time* to do it in?

Do yourself a favor; take the time. Sit down with your husband/wife, your children. Talk to your parents and close friends and ask all of them, *"What would we do if money weren't an issue? What would we do if we had all of the money we needed and the time to use it?"*

## BUILD YOUR "WHY" SO STRONG
## THAT NOTHING WILL STOP YOU!

You *will* face challenges in your new business, which at times will seem like insurmountable obstacles to your goals. You're going to have people tell you it can't be done. You'll have people tell you that even if it *could* be done, *you* will never be able to do it, *"so just give up."* But *those* people don't know your "WHY." Those are the same people who would have tried to stop you from saving your child on the other side of that beam.

Your "WHY" is not *their* "WHY," so they don't understand why you're willing to do what you're doing.

## IGNORE THEM, FOCUS ON YOUR "WHY"
## AND GO FOR YOUR DREAMS

You *are* going to have setbacks, gusts of wind sometimes as much as 60 miles an hour, and you may feel like you're falling. But if you have the focus, if you can keep your eyes on the prize as it were, you can regain your balance and make it across. Sometimes the ground will move between your legs and you'll look down and think about what will happen if you fall. But *don't*. Think of that person on the other side of the beam.

## WHAT IS THAT MAN HOLDING THAT IS SO
## PRECIOUS TO YOU THAT YOU WILL DO
## ANYTHING TO GET ACROSS?

Take a picture of it. Put it on the mirror in your bathroom, on the dashboard in your car, on your cubicle at work and even in your wallet. Keep it before you at all times and never *think* of the 3 steps behind you.

## JUST THINK *"WHY?... WHY AM I DOING THIS?"*
## AND THEN DO IT!

I still tell that story in my seminars and trainings even though the tragedy of 9/11 still haunts many people to this day. I do it out of respect to those who lost their lives on that day as well as to remind us all, that *anything* is in fact possible.

You see, back on August 6, 1974, a young 25-year-old man named Philippe Petit did the unthinkable. He secretly, and in fact illegally, stretched a tightrope wire across the two buildings and, for his own

"WHY," he walked across the 200-foot divide and accomplished the impossible.

My friend... So can YOU!

## About David

David Hull is best known for his humorous style of motivating and training in the Network Marketing Industry. As an author and comedic motivational speaker David has trained tens of thousands of people all over the world on how to create Loyalty, Fun & Profit in their home- based businesses. David's style of humor is all about telling stories and relating them to a lesson that can be used in business and in life.

David is a master in teaching people how to be able to communicate with anyone, anywhere and anytime, how to create urgency in one's business and how to create a powerful "Why" which will keep one going during the difficult times. People come from all over to learn to laugh at life for just a while and perhaps learn just the vital key that will take then to the next level in their business.

After 15 years of working for individual Network Marketing Companies, David has finally gone on his own. If you wish to learn more, see a sample of him on stage or have him speak at your event, you can learn more about David at: www.DavidHull-FinallyForSale.com

# CHAPTER 17

# Preparation and Balance – The Keys to WINNING

## By Sarah Loy

You can't put a price on *peace of mind*. We spend a large portion of our lives working to create wealth, but how much thought do we put into protecting what we've worked so hard for? Three common financial obstacles that people run into are: living too long, dying too soon, and experiencing various financial hardships along the way. Many of us don't think about these obstacles because they are uncomfortable to us. Others don't focus on them because these types of things overwhelm us. Although these are very serious issues, addressing them does not have to be complicated. "Winning" financially starts with being able to replace, guarantee, and/or protecting your income and savings.

Consider the following:

### I. Living Too Long

Americans feel more nervous and unprepared for their retirement today than in prior years. Right now there are 40 million senior citizens in the U.S. and by 2050 that number will more than double to almost 90 million. In the February 2012 issue of the Smithsonian, it stated that in 1950 there were 2,300 people over 100, and by 2050 there will be over 600,000. Surveys show that many are planning to work longer and are scaling

157

back their expectations of what their retirement will be. Retiring in "style" is harder than ever. According to a survey by Americans for Secure Retirement, 88% of all Americans are worried about "maintaining a comfortable standard of living in retirement."

People of all ages are concerned about putting away enough money for retirement. Many people get overwhelmed thinking about where to start. Luckily, when it comes to retirement planning, the best advice is often free and surprisingly simple. For example, "save early, save often, save consistently." It's easy to state but harder to implement. Few people actually stick to a rigorous savings schedule. Consider an automated savings program where contributions can be taken directly from your pay check or savings account. This will help you build a routine quicker than sporadically mailing a check. Don't delay getting started! As people spend more of their money each year instead of saving for retirement, we are seeing a growing number of people who are not able to stop working when they want. Certainly not with their desired lifestyle. According to the Employee Benefit Research Institute, 46% of all American workers have less than $10,000 saved for retirement. The longer you wait to save, the more money you are going to have to save each year to meet your goals.

By saving early, often, and consistently you can take advantage of the effect compound interest will have on your savings and investment goals. To quote Einstein, "Compounding is mankind's greatest invention, because it allows for the reliable, systematic accumulation of wealth." Compound interest is interest paid on interest. Your money makes money. It's a simple, yet effective way of building wealth. The only thing that's required of you is the discipline to leave your money alone and grow.

Two common pitfalls when planning for retirement are failing to diversify and underestimating the effects of inflation. Since no one really knows what the future will bring, it is important to diversify. Diversification spreads risk. Have you ever heard the phrase, "don't put all of your eggs in one basket." If one industry or sector suffers a loss, another may gain. A portfolio that is well diversified may sustain its value during market declines much better than one that is not.

Inflation can be the biggest risk to your retirement. Inflation is the sustained increase in the price of goods and services over time. Do you remember how much the cost of going to the movies, buying gas, or milk was twenty years ago? Can you imagine what they will be twenty years from today? If you are retired and living on a fixed income, you need to make sure that your investments earn more than the rate of inflation. One example is the cost of healthcare. Health care costs are rising faster than the rate of inflation. Current estimates project that the Medicare trust will be insolvent in 2017. Considering that almost 15% of the US will be 65 in 2017, it's clear that we need to save more and consider the value of a Medicare supplement plus long term care for meeting your retirement needs.

Everyone's facts and circumstances are different; don't leave your retirement to chance. Take a little time now to run the numbers – *your numbers*. However, doing this without an advisor usually results in missed investment opportunities, casual planning, and lax saving schedules. Working with an advisor can help you look at your "big picture" and help you build a plan that works with your philosophy and budget.

## II. Dying Too Soon

The subject of death, in general, makes most people uncomfortable. Nobody likes to think of themselves or their loved ones passing away. Most especially hate to think it could happen at an age younger than expected. This tends to be an area people file in their brain under: "It could never happen to me or anyone I know."

Luckily for my father, his parents discussed the uncomfortable scenario of an untimely death. I am sure when they purchased their first Life Insurance Policy they didn't think they would need it for a long time. Little did they know my grandfather would pass away when my dad was only fifteen years old and his brother was six. My grandmother was instantly a single, stay-at-home mother with two small children and no income. This small life insurance policy became their lifeblood. This money made all the difference to them. It allowed them to move from their military-owned house to a home of their own. It also allowed them to maintain a comfortable standard of living while my grandmother looked for employment. It also helped start a college fund for my dad, which was something my grandparents would have never been able to afford. Life insurance does not just provide finances for funerals and bills, life insurance provides options.

According to LIMRA's 2011 Life Insurance Ownership Survey, 41% of adults, an all-time low, are without any Life Insurance protection at all. What about the other 59%? The 2010 Survey revealed that half of U.S. households say they need more life insurance coverage. Even one-third of affluent households ($100,000+ income) lack sufficient coverage.

Just because an untimely death isn't an easy problem to think about, doesn't mean you should avoid it entirely, because it can actually be a simple problem to address. Do you currently own life insurance? If you do own life insurance, is it still enough? Life is constantly changing, so periodically reviewing to see if your current and future needs are protected, is crucial.

In the entire history of our agency, we have not had one widow or widower tell us the death benefit check they received was too large. There is no amount of money that can take away the pain or "replace" a loved one. However, receiving life insurance proceeds can give you time to heal. It can take away financial pressure during an emotional time.

## III. <u>Economic Hazards along the Way</u>

We are all aware that change is constant. Life will present you with obstacles from time to time. Preparing yourself ahead of time for challenges that can affect you and your family economically can help you lessen the severity or avoid the harmful impact all together.

The first place that you can assess your vulnerability and prevent unnecessary risk is by reviewing your Auto and Home Insurance with an insurance professional. Many people just think of these products as just another bill. Many people do not completely understand what they are paying for and why. Some people request "full coverage" only to find out their coverage doesn't feel very "full" at the time of claim. There are so many endorsements and coverage options available it is important to have an understanding of how protected you are, or aren't.

I found out the importance of understanding my coverages when I was 17. I was driving back to work and after coming from a complete stop, I hit another car. The accident happened at less than 5 miles per hour but the lady cut her lip on her cellphone. A few months later, four lawsuits showed up at our door and my parents and I were being sued for $100,000. The lawsuit did not list our insurance company like some people think it will. It listed our names. The guilt I felt was terrible. Luckily, my parents had planned properly and explained to me that the liability coverages they had purchased were high enough that we could sleep easy that night. We were able to send the lawsuits to our insurance company and definitely did not have to worry as much. This kind of feeling is priceless.

Another serious economic problem that many people are not properly prepared for, is becoming too sick or too hurt to work. What about you? If something happened to you today which kept you from going to work tomorrow, do you have proper plans to replace the income you will no longer be able to earn? Even if the disability is temporary, the side effects can be financially and emotionally devastating to you and your family.

To prepare for this kind of hurdle, or counteract it, you have a few options. At the time of disability, you could sell any assets you may own. This assumes that there is a market for your assets and that you are willing to part with things that you have worked a lifetime to accumulate. You could apply for Social Security, but benefits are generally not easy to qualify for. Assuming you do qualify, the benefits might not start right away or be enough to replace your earning power. You can, and should, start a savings account. Unfortunately, even if you save 10% of your income each year, it will still take you 10 years to set aside one year's income in reserves. A quick and economical way to counteract the effects of becoming too sick or too hurt to work is by purchasing a disability policy.

For example, a longtime friend of our family is Ted DiBiase, aka Pro Wrestling's Million Dollar Man. When Ted was at the top of his Pro Wrestling career, he had the opportunity to purchase a disability policy. At the time, he was successful, young and in great shape, and did not feel he needed the policy. However, his wife had the insight to talk Ted into purchasing the policy. Long story short, almost 1 year later, due to an injury in the wrestling ring, Ted had to stop wrestling and apply for disability. Because of the disability policy, he and his family were able to maintain their standard of living while successfully switching careers. Had he not listened to his wife and purchased that policy, he and his family could have lost everything.

Ultimately, it is important to maintain a healthy balance between accumulation – gaining more, and preservation – keeping what you already have. Luckily, you do not have to do this alone. There are plenty of professionals, like myself, that can help simplify complicated financial situations and concepts in way that you can understand and feel comfortable with.

Preparing for these three obstacles is a great start to having peace of mind and winning financially.

## About Sarah

Sarah Loy, FSS is a provider of "Peace of Mind." With over ten years experience in the insurance industry, her number one goal is to help clients protect what they value most. Through her Agency in Henderson, Nevada she performs professional insurance reviews to help build plans that fit into her clients philosophy and budget. Sarah believes that one size does <u>not</u> fit all and everyone should have the opportunity to build the future they want. Even if you never become an official client of her agency, Sarah always opens herself up as a resource and a safe-place to come with questions.

For more information and to contact Sarah, visit: sarahloy.com

# CHAPTER 18

# "Ask Yourself This..."

## By Andy Eilers, CRIS, CMC

*"There is one quality which one must possess to win, and that is definiteness of purpose, the knowledge of what one wants, and the burning desire to possess it."*

~Napoleon Hill

### AM I 'IN IT TO WIN IT' AND WILLING TO DO WHAT IT TAKES TO BE A CHAMPION?

In the summer of 2010, I had the opportunity to attend Tom Hopkins' 3-Day Boot Camp in Scottsdale, Arizona. Having read Tom's books and listened to his tapes over the years, I knew that going and experiencing his teaching in person would present an opportunity for that material to really come to life. Within a few minutes of Tom starting his instruction, I could see that the course was going to deliver everything I had expected.

One critical difference that I noticed right away between Tom's course and others I had attended over the years was the competition component. He tells the story at the beginning of the course about when he went to a sales seminar early in his career and committed to winning the sales competition there, which yielded a trophy that wasn't extravagant by any stretch of the imagination. However, it led to the decision by Tom to make his sales course a competition with a much more meaningful prize for the champion each year.

On the first day of the course, Tom reveals the prizes that are available to the top 10 students in terms of test scores for the entire course. The competition is split into two groups: Rookies (first year only) and Veterans (everyone else). The prizes for the winners consisted of beautiful glass trophies for places 2-10 in each group. As the grand prize for 1st place in each group, Tom awards an amazing lithograph about 2' high by 2' wide with an incredible full-color image of a Phoenix rising out of the fire and ashes. As he was explaining the competition and unveiled these two beautiful, professionally- framed portraits, I could feel my competitive juices begin to flow.

With hundreds of people attending, I remember looking around the room and thinking to myself, I can win this competition. I know how to listen intently to the material, study, internalize the material, and take exams with great results. As we began the course after this part, I stayed extremely focused on the task at hand. My goal was simple. I needed to get 100% on the two tests; equaling somewhere close to 40,000 points total, in order to have the best chance to walk out of that competition as the champion.

After hours of study that night following the classroom time, I felt ready to take the first of the two exams I now knew were coming. Once we had completed the first exam, we were asked to hand it to someone else to grade. My results were solid. I had earned 11,900 out of 12,000 possible points, missing only one word on the entire exam. Although I felt like I still had a chance to get the top prize, I was sure there were others in the room with perfect exam scores.

I remember thinking to myself that I would have to put even more time in the second night in order to really have the best chance. The challenge was that our group had been invited to have dinner with another group, mostly from Australia, and we didn't want to miss out on meeting with them. So I took the materials with me thinking that somehow I could break away from the group during that time, do whatever studying I could in pieces, and then finish my studying later that night. I quickly found that this strategy wasn't realistic as we were all talking and getting to know each other, which didn't allow me to focus on the material. I set the book down, enjoyed the time with them, and started studying again when I got back to the hotel.

At 3:00am, after another five hours of studying, I told myself I would get a few hours of sleep, wake up, and finish studying. Ah, the best laid plans, right? Well, I got up early, went through the material, and went into the exam knowing that I wasn't at my best. Have you ever felt that way going into an important meeting, a presentation, an exam, or maybe even a sporting event you were competing in? If you have, you know exactly what I am talking about. In this case, unprepared turned out to be unacceptable. Remember, results happen based on what you have done to produce them, good or bad.

Although I did well on the exam overall scoring in the top 10% of the group, I wasn't in the top 10. I remember congratulating the winners as I walked up to each of them separately. I remember feeling like I should have been one of them, but really knowing that I could have been the top one. After everyone had left the room, I went up to the stage, looked at all of the tables and the two easels which had held the lithographs up for everyone to see, and I made a commitment to myself that I would come back next year and win that competition!

In August of 2011, I did exactly that. I set my sights, got to the course early, didn't schedule anything for the evenings of the course so I could study, made sure I knew the material that Tom presented completely, which had been altered somewhat, and went into the exams each day with an expectation of no mistakes. I had the highest score available for the two exams combined, 41,800 points, which earned me the top award, "2011 Champion." It was an incredible experience walking up on stage and accepting that beautiful portrait from Tom, along with having him autograph the back and write "2011 Champion" on it. That portrait hangs on my wall in my office and I take great pride in all of the hours of study, focus, energy, effort, and mostly, the belief in myself that I could accomplish this and did. I plan to return in 2012 and put everything I have into repeating as champion. Is there a goal in your life that you have a second chance to achieve? Are you willing to pay the price to do so? Ultimately, you need to have a conversation with yourself and be willing to do everything necessary that many others, before and after you, aren't willing to do in order to achieve what you have chosen to achieve. Say it out loud: "I am responsible for my life and the results I create!"

Surround yourself with other successful people anytime you can. They take responsibility too! Make time to immerse yourself in learning from the best trainers and mentors you can find. This could be a few hours, a few days, or even a week at a time if the material will improve your life. Remember, to be a champion at anything, you must be willing to invest time and resources in yourself. As a professional, recognize the talent and skills you can develop by learning from great sales trainers like Tom Hopkins. It will change your life in the same way it has changed mine. *Be in it to win it!*

## HOW DO I APPROACH A "SALE" WITH PEOPLE I WANT TO DO BUSINESS WITH?

I have found that when I create acronyms like this one for "**SALE**" to breakdown words, it makes them easier for people to remember and use successfully. "**S**" is for *Set up the Opportunity*; "**A**" is for *Ask Qualifying Questions*; "**L**" is for *Lead to a Winning Decision*; "**E**" is for *Execute the Transaction*.

In looking at this more closely, starting with the "**S**" in this acronym, consider how you are currently going about *Setting up the opportunity* to get in front of a future client if it's for new business you are creating, or for repeat business with current people, companies, or families you serve, to keep the business. I have found that if I am planning on meeting with someone for something that may appear to benefit me more than it benefits them, that being respectful of their time and situation is paramount. With that in mind, call the individual in advance to set a time that allows you to visit with them regarding the matter you need to discuss, so that they can appropriately make that time available for you when you arrive.

Once you have arrived, invest a few minutes inquiring about how they are doing with sincere concern for them and their family/business/situation whenever possible. Your plan should then be to proceed to "**A**" in the acronym, which is to *Ask qualifying questions*. These questions should be focused in areas that are valuable to assessing their needs, which should start with their values about your product or service. Is it something they already own or are you creating a need for something new to them? Once you know this, you can proceed to confirm the true value they put in owning your product or service.

Second, you should find out whether or not you have competitors offering the same product or service to them. I believe that professional people should not "quote for practice" in order to keep a current vendor or person they do business with honest. In my opinion, that leads to an extremely low closing ratio, low hourly rate of income to the person, reduced profit to his or her organization, and a lot of wasted time and energy.

Unless there is some incredible benefit your product or service brings that the client recognizes as such, and not you, if the client is shopping for value, you will simply fall in line based on that total investment amount – not necessarily what you perceive as the better value. You then need to find out if they are comfortable or afflicted in their current situation with a similar product or service.

If there is no pain, the likelihood of them moving to you for the same thing is low. However, if there is pain or other issues they would like to resolve, you need to know what it is so you can offer a solution to it. One of my favorite sayings that I heard many years ago regarding this is, "Comfort the afflicted and afflict the comfortable."

Finally, you need to set some guidelines about when they will make a decision, who will be involved, what their budget is to own the product or service, and that if you are able to provide the best solution within their budget that you will earn the business. Remember, the client will ultimately own a product or service for his or her reasons, not yours.

Next you should move to "L" and focus on *Leading the individual or group to a winning decision*. This is where you have to be honest with yourself and them about what you are offering versus what is available by owning someone else's product or service, or not owning the product or service at all. In many cases, for example, in the field of insurance, there is a renewal date for a product.

This makes it easier for a current or future client to plan for the event of owning again and again. It also allows clients to decide how they are going to approach owning the product each year, and proceed accordingly.

However, if this is something new to them that doesn't have a set date where they need to complete everything by, it is easy to allow distraction of everything else in their lives to paralyze the action of owning your offering.

You should have asked the questions by this point to know what you have to do to earn the business. Now you need to follow through and either offer the solution they told you they want within the budget they provided for you, or be honest with them about the fact that you can't. Either way, you can do what you need to do and move on to the next step, which is offering a solution or walking away professionally.

If you are going to stay involved in the transaction and believe you do have the solution that they are looking for, you should now move to "**E**" and *Execute the transaction*. This step can happen in many different ways, and sometimes over multiple steps. The part that many people miss in this step, which I believe costs them transactions over and over, is the review.

Start by going over everything that has been discussed with regards to what they were looking for, what their values are, any competitive products or services that they are looking at along with yours, current pain and/or improvement they are looking for in a new situation that includes you (whether a current or future client), and confirmation of the guidelines set in your last meeting or call. Once you have done all of this and feel comfortable you have a legitimate shot to earn the business, now you can proceed to the executing the transaction.

If you have paperwork they need to approve that allows you to execute the transaction, get it done. If you need to collect an initial amount and set up monthly installments for the rest, get it done. If you need to collect the total amount in order to proceed, get it done. At this point, you should be formalizing the transaction, not hoping that you are in the game and planning to dazzle them with your selling skills. Professional people make it happen by staying focused on other people's needs, not their own. This gives them the best chance to know when a transaction is going to happen and when it's not.

So as you move through the individual letters of the "**SALE**" acronym, it is important to stay focused and complete each letter successfully before moving on to the next. Again, **Set up the opportunity**, **Ask qualifying questions**, **Lead to a winning decision**, and **Execute the transaction**. By taking each opportunity one letter at a time like this, you also put yourself in a position where you can evaluate whether you want to proceed to the next letter or not. If you don't have a legitimate shot to earn the business, regardless of the reason, why are you there?

You are a professional and you deserve to be paid for your work, right? Don't let yourself be hypnotized by what appears to be an opportunity, but is really a black hole for your time, resources, energy, and effort. You are better than that! Follow this acronym one letter at a time, execute more transactions, and be the best you can be for yourself and all of those who are counting on you. **Be in it to win it!**

## About Andy

Andy Eilers, CRIS is the Director of Sales & Marketing for First Service Insurance in Roseville, California. First Service specializes in construction and transportation insurance in multiple states with over 2,000 current and active clients. With over 20 years of sales, sales management, and sales training experience with a multitude of companies, Andy's goal is to assist people and companies in achieving their personal and professional goals – through teaching, managing, training, and personal and professional coaching. For over 20 years, he has studied the material of many of the great trainers and teachers of our time including: Tom Hopkins, Brian Tracy, Zig Ziglar, and Napoleon Hill. He has earned top sales and sales management awards throughout his career. Andy is also the reigning "Champion" of the Tom Hopkins 3-Day Boot Camp held annually in Scottsdale, Arizona. In addition, Andy has consulted for many companies in the areas of motivation and sales training throughout Northern California.

Andy has a BA in Economics, with a minor in Communication Studies from CSU Sacramento. He will complete his MA in Psychology with an emphasis in Organizational and Business Psychology this year. Andy plans to begin his Doctor of Psychology program in 2013. Andy is also in the process of completing an audio program including all of his "Ask Yourself This…" material and other sales and motivational instructional information. Andy is an accomplished martial artist holding a 1st degree black belt in Tae Kwon Do. He is also an avid reader, golfer, tennis player, singer, poet, and wine enthusiast.

For more information on Andy Eilers, email him at:
andy@firstserviceweb.com or
love2live@mac.com.

CHAPTER 19

# Internet Sales Strategy for Real Estate Success

## By Dennis DeSouza

Working with the luxury homebuyer obtained through the Internet can be one of the most rewarding experiences. First off, you gain a new client that has access to other potential buyers and sellers that are in the same wealth level. The other obvious plus is that you stand to earn a very sizeable commission. The wealthy luxury homebuyer typically has a number of friends who are interested in purchasing Real Estate, and because you are referred by one of their like-minded friends, they are more likely not only to use you, but to also stay loyal to you. The wealthy run in the same circles and have common interests. Of course, the majority of our Internet homebuyers are looking in the $400,000 to $2,000,000 range, but an increasing number are in the higher price ranges.

Now a good 80% of my buyer clients are generated through the Internet, with the other 20% coming from past clients/referrals and office walk-ins. My office is located in a very high traffic location with direct street frontage. I highly recommend being in an office that has walk-in traffic! It is a huge advantage to an agent to have this added source of leads. Now to internet leads - I come across agents every day that swear Internet leads are horrible, but I can tell you with absolute certainty that this statement could not be further from the truth. I have sold hundreds of millions of dollars of Real Estate strictly from Internet leads. Now these leads are not free to generate, and once generated, they must be followed up correctly and diligently or they will go to waste and another agent will end up reaping the rewards. An example of the current clients I am working with that were obtained through my Internet marketing strategies range from several CEO's of major US corporations who are looking for vacation homes in the San Diego region, as well as high-level executives that are being relocated to the region. These buyers are looking in the $2,000,000 to $40,000,000 price range. That is not a typo! The Internet will find you buyers in that price range more often than you think.

If I told you the names of some of these folks you would be very surprised since they are well known in the media. Fortunately, the average agent does not think it's possible to generate leads like these since they believe that, "those types of buyers do not search on the Internet or contact an agent that way." This could not be further from the truth! I am just extremely thankful most agents think this way – less competition for me! Granted, the time cycle is longer than average for buyers in this price range, and many do not end up purchasing, however when you run the numbers, you will realize that you do not need to sell many of these to make a small fortune.

Early on, I realized a few key distinctions with regards to luxury Internet leads. They usually leave good contact numbers to reach them, they obviously have the means to make such purchases, and this is the big one, they are easier to deal with as long as you know how to deal with them and interact with them the way they want to be interacted with. Remember these people are just like you and me and truly act very similar to the average homebuyer.

The luxury buyer is typically looking for a home that represents a good value. They did not become wealthy by overpaying! They also usually want a home that has been remodeled already – which sometimes poses a challenge in that it may not be remodeled to their tastes. These high end buyers usually do not want to tackle a remodel project since they are busy folks and use these homes for as little as a week per year. They usually want turnkey or close to turnkey without a ton of work needed to be done. In fact if the furnishings are nice and to their liking they will often ask for the furnishings to be included in the sale. One other common distinction is that they prefer to be contacted by email. However, your first contact should always be by phone so you can get a good idea of their needs. When you speak to someone either in person or on the phone, you will pick up subtle points that an email message just will not provide to you. Despite what anyone tells you, if you do not have a legitimate phone number for the client, your chances of selling a home to them drop to under 5%! In a nutshell, working with this type of client is a special experience. They are typically very thankful for your service, and they are willing to refer their friends and colleagues to you provided you have represented them properly. First and foremost, you have to do an outstanding job for them.

Now let me get into the meat and potatoes of the process we use for our Internet strategy. Here we will cover what type of website to use to attract our high-end buyers, the buying of the leads and most importantly, the follow up. This is the critical component that thankfully is done poorly or not done at all by other agents! Again less competition for me. So here we go. First off, you need a website that does a great job at conversion. Your website should not have your photos plastered all over it since this will kill the conversion. You want a website that "flies under the radar" – in other words one that does not scream "real estate agent." No one wants to deal with or get bothered by a real estate agent, all they want is the information. Let me repeat – all they want is the information.

Buyers and sellers actually want two things and only two things when searching on the Internet. They want selection and convenience. Your website should address both of these and must do it well, or they will click off your site and move onto the next one! Selection and convenience should be key features of the site. As stated earlier, a good conversion site needs to fly under the radar, be able to have the buyer or seller search homes (selection) and be convenient (easy to use and navigate). A good site should convert at 10 to 15% –meaning out of every 100 hits, you will get 10 to 15 leads. A "branded" site with agent and brokerage photos and logos everywhere will convert at about 3 to 5%. In other words, your ROI (return on investment) triples simply by having a non-branded web site. You also must require a phone number on the sign up page. Not doing so will waste 99% of your money. Again, if you cannot call the prospect, your chances of closing a deal with them drop to under 5%. If anyone tells you otherwise, they have no clue as to what they are talking about, and are likely trying to sell you one of their inferior sites. Ask me how I know – been there, done that!

You can buy the leads in a variety of ways. You can do Pay Per Click (PPC) through the most common channels such as Google Ad words or you can use resellers like Homegain. I chose the former as it is more efficient. With Homegain, you do not have to do the key words as they just deliver leads for a dollar amount. In my area the average cost per lead is $23. So you can clearly see that follow up and ultimately conversion are paramount in being an effective internet agent or you will go broke quickly. Most agents try the internet route but fail for reasons that will become more obvious as we move forward.

Once a lead signs up on the site, it is very important to get back to them as quickly as possible. But I caution you, do not try to wing it – always use a script! Do not call them when you cannot speak clearly and without distractions. Also, I highly recommend using a hands-free headset so you have freedom of movement with your hands to write or type notes as you speak to the lead. You are in a "dog show" and every misstep will cost you! I am a firm believer in scripts, as are all other mega agents around the country. Your script should address their needs and wants and more importantly their timing. I have seen it over and over where agents get stuck on a call because they are winging it. This is a very common mistake that will cost you sales and profits. By all means always use a script! Your main goal when speaking with a lead is to get a face-to-face appointment. When you pick up the phone your goal is to meet with the buyer, show them your value and sign them to a buyer's broker agreement.

Your presentation should always be scripted as well. We utilize PowerPoint presentations when meeting a buyer on the initial consultation. It shows the benefits of working with us in an easy-to-follow presentation. Once we go through the presentation, the likelihood of them signing a buyer broker agreement increases dramatically, and we are able to convert 80% of our appointments into signed buyer clients. This will commit the buyer to working with us exclusively and allow us to pour our heart and soul into finding them the perfect home on their terms. Once they commit to us, we know we will ultimately be compensated for our efforts. Surprisingly, the only agents that have an issue with signing buyer broker agreements are the agents that have been in the business for years. The newer agents do not have any issue pulling out this document and getting it signed. They do not know any other way, whereas experienced agents do not think the buyers will sign. This makes no sense, but that is the way it is.

When you are starting your Internet strategy, you will be the one making the calls at first and, depending on your goals, you may consider hiring an inside sales agent. An Inside Sales Agent is basically a person that follows up with the leads and books appointments. I will refer to the Inside Sales Agent as an "ISA" Every agent in the country that does large volumes of transactions usually has 1 to 4 ISAs. Obviously you need to generate dozens of leads per day to justify an ISA, but it can be one of the best moves you will make. This is a more advanced strategy for the larger producers, but one that should be considered by the ambitious agent. Currently we have 2 full time ISAs that book appointments for all of our agents on my team.

Another strategy that we have implemented is that we do not pass out any leads to our agents until the buyer is ready to meet with us or to look at homes. We have been down this road before and to be blunt the agents are absolutely horrible at follow up! Our process is that the ISAs will "own" or "be responsible for" the lead up to the day that the buyer is physically ready to meet for the consultation, or ready to see a home. Agents cannot possibly handle all of the daily activities they must perform and then be expected to follow up with an abundance of leads. Like I said, this takes two fulltime ISAs to handle the follow up properly and not let leads fall through the cracks. I cannot stress this enough. Once you get to the point of generating the sheer number of leads I am referring to, I strongly recommend hiring your first ISA.

Now if the lead cannot come in to meet or is from out of town, we will ask them when they are planning on coming into town. Once we get that information, we would ask them when a good time to follow up with them would be. Whatever time frame they tell us, we cut in half. In other words, if they say to call back in 6 months we will call them back in 3 months. You would be shocked at how reliant successful Real Estate sales is on timing. We have been burned countless times because the timing was off. By cutting the time frame they tell you in half, your odds of conversion increase exponentially.

Another strategy that is highly effective once you gather enough leads is to do email blasts to your lists. Of course, the most obvious blast you should do is to match your Internet buyers with your personal listings. This might sounds obvious, but you would be surprised at how many agents do not use this technique. Of course the larger your database, the more effective this strategy is. For example, we have over 50,000 Internet leads in our system, so you could imagine that our targeted email blast showcasing our listings is highly effective in promoting our client's home. We also send out blasts to our database with the offer of a "Free list of Distressed Homes" or a "Best Buys" list. This will stir the pot a bit and get some of the leads to raise their hands that may have been dormant in the past. This yet again gives us another opportunity to interact with them. You want to make the offer in the following manner. Let the lead know that you are compiling a list of best buys and that you will have this ready by "X" date and if it is OK, you will get it to them by "Y" date. This will let the lead know that you are actually doing some work for them, and this often times will generate a positive response that speaks to their timing. They might come out and tell you that they are still 'a ways out' and to hold off on the list for now. Others will tell you they want the list ASAP. These are the ones to hone in on like a laser, since the likelihood of them making a purchase is higher.

Once again, I want to stress that your main goal when contacting an Internet lead is to get a face-to-face appointment. This is how to increase your sales in a big way. It is much too easy to chit-chat and not close for the appointment. The mega-agents across the country understand this concept very clearly. You want to be face-to-face in a buyer consultation and you want the buyer to commit to your services in writing. This not only gives you security that the buyer will work with you exclusively, but also gives the buyer the promise of great representation. If the buyer does not commit to any one agent, every agent they deal with will be trying to sell them every house they show them. We would rather have a firm commitment from the buyer and then we will show them as many homes as it takes since we know they are committed to us. Pretty simple distinction – but one that makes quite a bit of sense!

In summary, you want to generate the Internet lead through an "unbranded" site that has a great conversion rate. Next, you want to make sure you follow up with them as quickly as possible, as this will increase your odds of speaking with them. Once you speak with them, your goal is to get them to a face-to-face meeting with you so you can go over your presentation. Once this is done you want to have them commit to only working with you as their agent. You do this by having them sign a "Buyers Broker" agreement. Once you have the agreement signed, you are ready 'to work your tail off' to find them the right house and at their terms. If you follow these simple steps you will be sure to increase your sales ten fold!

Well, this is our Internet strategy that we developed that has proved very effective for me. I hope that this lesson helps other colleagues throughout the country and world improve their businesses and income! The Internet is a very powerful tool for many businesses including Real Estate. If done properly, your Internet strategy could be one of the most important parts of your business and one that will become a larger part of your overall strategy. The Internet lead is truly a blessing to me and I hope you will find the same success that we have experienced over the years.

## About Dennis

For the past several years, La Jolla-based REALTOR®, Dennis DeSouza, has ranked among the top 30 real estate agents in San Diego County—out of more than 5,000 licensed REAL-TORS®. With a team of highly-skilled real estate agents and support staff, DeSouza Select Properties is one of the top producing teams in the nation. RE/MAX recently awarded DeSouza his third Diamond Award, which is the most prestigious award in the RE/MAX family, and is given to less than 100 agents each year.

DeSouza has also been consistently recognized as one of the top 100 agents with RE/MAX, out of well over 70,000 RE/MAX agents nationwide.

Describing his business philosophy, DeSouza recently commented:—
"Our systems are constantly improving each year. I am eager to learn what other top agents in the country are using to market homes, and to adopt the most successful systems into my business. For our buyers, we strive to save our clients money when they find the home they want to purchase, and for our sellers, our selling team receives continuous training on effective negotiation. These skills have saved our clients hundreds of thousands of dollars in price negotiations over the years.

With constant improvements, our systems continue to be highly efficient in selling our clients' properties, as well as in locating homes for our buyer clients.

I feel that when the market gets more difficult, it opens up an amazing opportunity to gain market share. In real estate, you must always be improving and delivering the highest service possible to your clients in order to be successful. You not only have to provide the absolute best service to survive in this industry, but you must also net your sellers more money, as well as negotiate on behalf of your buyers. Good service is not good enough any more!"

Dennis DeSouza and his team are located in the Birdrock area of La Jolla, California.

# CHAPTER 20

# Eight (8) Steps to Building an Outstanding Team Which Provides World Class Customer Service

## By Jamey Hopper

Driving down a dark and lonely road one night far from any sign of civilization, Mrs. Smith had a one-car accident. Her car ended up in a ditch beside the road. Though she suffered only a few minor injuries she was pinned in her car. She began to panic as she realized she could not escape and her car could not be seen from the road. Mrs. Smith frantically tried to reach assistance with her cell phone. With growing worry, she realized she was in a remote area and her cell service was weak at best. The only success she had at reaching a live voice was when calling her husband's office, she reached their answering service. The efficient operator quickly contacted emergency assistance and Mr. Smith. The operator then returned to the line and chatted with Mrs. Smith until assistance arrived. The remarkable part of this story is that the operator handling this call so admirably was only in her third week of employment at the answering service.

It is a rare but wonderful occasion when an employee takes exactly the right steps to overwhelm a customer with caring and superior service. It is even more inspiring when the employee providing the service is brand new. It is possible to build, or re-build, an organization committed to superlative service and to attract employees committed to that purpose. Many books have been written about this subject. Two of the best I have found are <u>Good to Great</u> by Jim Collins and <u>Mastering the Rockefeller Habits</u> by Verne Harnish. Using material in these two books as a starting point, I followed the steps outlined below to build an organization with superlative service.

Our management team began the process in the fall of 2008 on the company I had purchased in 1989. At that time service was good, but not great. Growth was good, but not great. Our company culture was satisfactory, but probably short of good. Profitability was acceptable, but, well you get the picture. I challenged our management team to rebuild the company changing our attitude and performance from good to great.

We immediately began the process of evaluating, improving, rejecting, redesigning and reformulating virtually every system, policy, procedure and process at our company. The work is far from complete, yet the results have already been dramatic. I am convinced that by following the eight steps capsuled below, any organization can be built to provide world-class customer service. It is not an easy task and takes total commitment from company owners and executive management. If the steps are followed the results are gratifying and immensely profitable.

### I. Establish the Goal

Create a *Big Hairy Audacious Goal* (from Jim Collins in <u>Built to Last</u>) – What defines long-term success for you and the company? Set your sights high and then establish your goal higher still! Make sure everyone in the organization feels a part of this goal. Be certain that the goal states the purpose of the company. The purpose is a higher calling, a compelling vision of a future each employee can desire. With the right long term goal and purpose, employees are not coming to work every day, they are fulfilling their mission in life. This step begins the company on a journey to create energy, improve attendance, reduce turnover and amaze customers with incredible levels of service.

## II. Identify the Values

Some company owners establish or create their own set of Core Values. For new companies this obviously makes sense. In my view, it is impossible for existing companies to create Core Values because they are usually already established. Identify the Core Values that are present in your company. Do nothing if they are in line with the long term goal. If they are not in line with the long term goal, then set about growing new values. Find the key players within your company that best exemplify the values that are aligned with your goal and purpose, and begin hiring, training and coaching to surround them with like-minded employees.

Our company followed the steps recommended by Verne Harnish in his book <u>Mastering the Rockefeller Habits</u> to identify our Core Values in the fall of 2008. Two years later our Culture Committee spent several months reconsidering, debating, re-evaluating and dissecting our Core Values. We agreed that we had done fairly well the first time but we did make one minor change. Companies and cultures change over time. Core Values probably will change very little. But perhaps the understanding or definition of the values can change. This happened at our company.

## III. Build the Culture

As Tony Hsieh described in his outstanding book <u>Delivering Happiness,</u> having a unified, clear and functional corporate culture can be fundamental to a company's success. Cultures that happen by accident are rarely part of a long term success story. Cultures that are built to drive cohesive, compelling and fulfilling work relationships craft their own opportunities for success. With a Big Hairy Audacious Goal created to focus every employee's sights on a future of learning, growth, superiority and dominance of a marketplace, motivation is built into the corporate culture. *Make culture a part of every hire and fire decision.* Never let a single employee with a negative attitude bring down the psyche of their team. As Jim Collins described in <u>Good to Great</u>, all companies must fire workers who do not fit the company culture; the Great companies succeed because they fire them sooner.

We created a Culture Committee, made up of members of management and front line employees in equal numbers. We brought in consultants to lead our team through the process. We met for approximately two hours twice per month, with some additional homework assignments, for approximately one year. During this time we were able to assess our current status, review our Core Values, re-write our Mission Statement, explore our Company Vision, create a Strategic Plan and begin implementation of the Strategic Plan. Each step was vital to the overall success of the committee, and to the success the company has experienced these past three years.

## IV. Craft the Plan

Form an Executive Team of key managers. The newly formed Executive Team must meet regularly to create short-term plans and goals and to establish the measurements for which success is recognized. This is all put together in a Strategic Plan. Our team created a plan for 2009 as we launched our new initiative. We then review and renew the plan quarterly. The Executive Team sets the quarterly priorities and the frontline employees set the specific goals. Operating under the principle "We Support That Which We Help Create" has enhanced our ability to both stretch and reach our goals each quarter. Early in the process, the Executive Team set the goals and they were rarely achieved. When we asked the employees to set the goals, they set them even higher than the Executive Team had, but we began reaching the higher goals. *There is no doubt that securing "buy in" from all employees by making them a part of the planning and goal setting process is fundamental to achieving success.*

## V. Design or Re-design the Systems

With great people motivated to do fabulous work, many company systems must be redesigned to accommodate the new levels of performance. Employee recruiting must be re-focused to ensure the ability to find superstars. New interview questions and methods must be developed to attract the stars and repel the pretenders. In the same way, operating systems and procedures must be reviewed and renewed to allow the superstars to flourish. This step especially will be continuous throughout the process.

Perhaps the most important systems of all relate to internal (with employees) and external (with customers, prospective customers, vendors, etc.) communication. *To meet or exceed a customer's expectations, you must do what you say you will do.* Missing a promised contact point in resolving a customer complaint is usually more irritating than the original service concern. Failure to properly follow up with all job applicants, even if you have so many an automated response is required, is just one example of poor external communications.

A company bulletin board, Intranet, newsletter or gossip chain is no substitute for systematic, effective communication. Regular meetings including daily department huddles, weekly department meetings, weekly management team meetings, monthly company meetings, quarterly planning meetings, etc., go a long way to ensuring excellent internal communications. Yet designing and implementing additional systems that work best within your company is vital to unleash the power of your employees.

## VI. Train for Superiority

All companies include training as a part of their routine operations. *It is no coincidence that the most successful companies have the best training programs.* Employees are motivated and empowered by acquiring tools for operational success. Create a Mindset (see Carol Dweck's book by that name) of personal and corporate growth throughout the organization. Training cannot only take place at the beginning of employment; training must become a fundamental part of the company culture. A Beat The Boss reading contest is just one example of a tool to keep both boss and employees focused on learning and personal growth.

We experienced our greatest success when we created a customized training plan for each employee. Every employee, their direct supervisor and the training department were all focused on the activities necessary for growth and success. By having a written plan with specific goals and deadlines there was no question of the expectations from those participating in the process: supervisor, trainer and trainee. With a clear vision of their opportunity for growth and development, employees became more focused, engaged and energized.

## VII. Coach for Success

A fundamental part of creating the growth Mindset is coaching and mentoring throughout the organization. Encourage all managers to make the transition from Boss to Coach. This step has been the least visible in our success, yet perhaps the most important. Simply asking the right questions allows the boss to empower the employee to seek their own solutions. *Fundamental to this effort is encouraging the employee to spend time enhancing their greatest strength rather than struggling to improve a weakness.* Merely bringing an employee's weakness up to average is good enough, but improving an employee's strength allows a company to flourish.

Working with an executive coach over the years has been extremely beneficial to me. Yet even more beneficial was when I began to coach employees myself. It surprised me to discover I learned and developed even more through coaching than being coached. A great lesson for life is to adopt the tenet "the more you give, the more you get." This has especially been my experience with coaching.

## VIII. Step Back, Evaluate and Start Again

*Evaluation could be considered the first or the last step of the process.* Just as it is impossible to take a journey without knowing the ending point, it is also impossible to take a journey without knowing the beginning. I wrote this starting with the end and ending with the beginning. The success process is really a circle and not a straight line.

The evaluation step must include input from employees and customers. A great tool for surveying your employees is described in the book 12: The Elements of Great Managing. Using this tool allows the measurement of your employees against some of the standards described in the book. Another essential tool is for the chief executive to meet regularly with all employees, or conduct focus groups of employees if size dictates, to solicit their frank point of view.

There are many ways to gain insight from your customers and be sure to include focus groups, surveys and especially Social Media. Your customers are already talking about you in Social Media. Fail to join them at your peril.

**Once you discover the state of mind of your employees and customers, it is time to begin anew the process of building your company**.

Good Luck!

## About Jamey

Jamey is the owner and President of Dexcomm, a Telephone Answering Service and Call Center based in Louisiana, a position he has held since 1989.

Dexcomm has been awarded Gold Level Site Certification from ATSI, has won the ATSI Award of Excellence for eight consecutive years, and the CAMX Award of Excellence for all four years it has participated in the program. Dexcomm is one of the very few services in the country to hold all three awards simultaneously. Dexcomm has averaged approximately 12% annual growth since 1992. For the first two years of the program, in 2011 and 2012, Dexcomm has been named to the LSU 100, representing the fastest growing businesses owned or managed by a graduate of Louisiana State University.

Jamey has served as President and Board Member of several Telephone Answering Service industry associations. He has made numerous presentations at industry conferences, usually on the subjects of Sales and Marketing or Customer Service. He is currently leading a series of Customer Service Webinars for the Southern Telemessaging Association.

Jamey received his bachelor's degree in Economics from Vanderbilt University. He received an MS in Finance and an MBA from Louisiana State University.

Jamey worked as a Commercial Loan Officer at a bank, a Hospital Administrator, a medical office manager and a small business management consultant before purchasing Dexcomm.

Jamey's passions are his wife, his church, his dogs, his work, his 26 nieces and nephews, his LSU Tigers and Customer Service. To learn more about providing outstanding service to your customers please visit: www.dexcomm.com.

# CHAPTER 21

# Are You Growing Your Business? ...Or Going Out Of Business!

## By Ong Whatt Kim

*"Success is the sum of small efforts,*
*repeated day in and day out."*

~ Robert Collier

If you truly want to be "in it to win it," you have to really look hard at the big picture of your business. Without a comprehensive analysis from all relevant angles, you risk a critical weakness of your business model making itself known at precisely the wrong time - and threatening your very viability.

I'm very grateful that my almost forty years of experience in business sales, marketing, training and consulting has given me many important insights into business success – and what it truly takes to win in the marketplace, no matter what industry you're in.

In this chapter, I want to share my hard-earned knowledge – and give you the tools to:

- Create a vibrant vision for your business

- Identify specific strategies to enable ongoing growth and success

- Use the proven P.E.S.T. and T.O.W.S. analytic models to "road-test" your business

- Put into action a powerful Idea Generation Process

So – let's get started!

## I. CREATING YOUR BUSINESS VISION

Your vision for your business defines everything you do – and it must take into account many factors to be sustainable. You must answer the following questions in an honest and a complete way, and those answers must be reflected back into that vision.

**Question 1: What do you intend to achieve in your business?**
Where do you want this business to go? Do you want to keep it small and manageable? Do you want to grow it into a larger enterprise? Do you want it to be a local, national or international business? Understanding what you want to achieve with your business will guide you as you build it.

**Question 2: Who is this business for?**
Are you in this business for yourself? Is it a partnership with a friend? Are you doing it for your family? If you are not primarily doing it for yourself, will you have enough of an emotional investment in its success?

**Question 3: What is your purpose for this business?**
Is this meant to be a side business – or do you see this as becoming your primary business venture? Do you want to become a leader in your business community? Or do you just want to make as much money as you can?

**Question #4: What ultimate rewards are you after?**
Every business person has different goals they want to achieve from a company. You may be looking to build a business that runs itself – or you may want to be the hands-

on architect of a business empire. Look at what you personally want from your business and target it accordingly.

**Question #5: What kind of resources will you need?**

Some businesses literally only require a computer and an Internet connection, while others require a great deal of financing, infrastructure and staffing to really be viable. You must make sure you have what you need to make your particular business a success – or you will find yourself fighting a battle you don't have the weapons to win.

**Question #6: What additional skills do you require?**

A new business requires a lot of knowledge and training that you may not possess. That means you either have to gain that knowledge and training or be able to hire those who do. There is no harm in admitting what you don't know; there is harm in making fatal mistakes by proceeding out of ignorance.

**Question #7: What is your definition of success?**

Many of the preceding questions have hinted at this final one – because this is the most important. Your definition of success might mean creating an ongoing business to employ your family members, making enough money so you can retire, or becoming a respected business mogul that will give you power and influence.

## II. DEVELOPING GROWTH STRATEGIES

If you have your vision for your future business in place, your next step should be to develop specific strategies for your company's growth and development. Those strategies should center on where you will be making your revenue – your customers.

There are only three basic types of customers - **Existing Customers** (those who are already buying from you), **Potential Customers** (those you must convert to buying from you), and **Lost Customers** (those who have bought from you, but no longer do). All three customer categories have the potential of increasing your revenue, if you understand how to market to them.

You may believe that, since **Existing Customers** are already spending money with you, you don't need to bother to continue to sell to them. That's a huge missed opportunity. These people already trust your company, or they wouldn't be buying from you. You can capitalize on that trust, by attempting to increase their number of orders, increase the average size of their orders, or offer additional products that they haven't bought from you yet. *The important thing is to not take them for granted, but continue to develop strong relationships with them.* You will always lose some existing customers along the way, but you want to keep your retention rate as high as possible.

**Potential Customers** can be the most expensive ones to market to, because you have to start from scratch to acquire them. Therefore, it's important to put in place ongoing processes of continually acquiring new and viable leads with which you have the opportunity to convert to customers. It doesn't matter how little they order from you at the start, the point is to get your foot in the door and establish a relationship with them that can blossom. *Always make sure you are delivering everything you promise in that initial sale, or you will never have a chance to regain their trust.*

Many business people forget about their **Lost Customers**, wrongly assuming that they will never buy from them again. *Keep in mind that if they bought from you once, chances are good that they will again.* Whatever circumstances motivated them to buy from someone else may have changed again, and in the meantime, they may have simply forgotten about you. It's always worth trying to sell to them again.

Most businesses make the mistake of only going after Potential Customers, ignoring Lost and Existing Customers, even though the most revenue opportunities usually lie within the latter two groups. Keep that in mind as you develop your growth strategies.

## PUT YOUR BUSINESS TO THE "P.E.S.T."

Another important step when looking at your business from all possible angles is to see how outside forces might impact it, either in a negative or a positive way. The P.E.S.T. analysis is a wonderful way to do just that - and you'll find a diagram of it below.

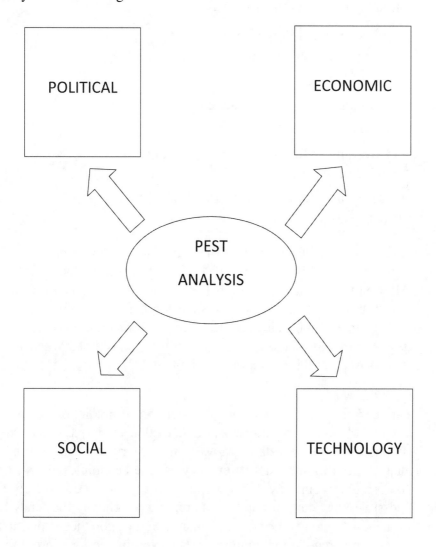

Let's take a look at the four main elements of the P.E.S.T. analysis and see what sorts of business issues they bring up.

## • POLITICAL

As we all have seen in our experiences, the political climate of the countries we do business in can definitely affect how profitable we can be. Governments intervene in economies to various extents - so examine how that intervention impacts your particular industry in the following ways:

Ecological and Environmental issues

- Regulatory Bodies and Processes

- Trading Policies

- Funding Grants and Initiatives

- Government Policies

- Government Terms and Pending Changes in Leadership

- Home and International Market Lobbying Groups

- Wars and Internal Conflicts

The basic type of government that's in place must also be taken into account. How stable is it? Is there freedom of the press? How entrenched and difficult is the bureaucracy to deal with? Is competition encouraged, or are state-run businesses the norm? What legislation is being debated? How strict is the employment regulation? All of these factors should be considered when it comes to fine-tuning your business model.

## • ECONOMIC

In 2005, few if any were paying attention to predictions of a severe worldwide economic crash. In late 2008, everyone was paying attention to the devastating downturn that struck us all. You may not be able to accurately foretell what the economic winds may be bringing your way, but you can try to assess as completely as possible what current conditions are, and which way they may be heading. Try to get the best information you can on these important economic areas in the countries where you intend to or are doing business:

- Inflation and Interest Rates

- Unemployment, Labor Supply and Labor Costs

- Disposable Income and Wealth Distribution
- Globalization
- International trends
- Taxation issues, both general and specific to your products and services
- Market and Trade cycles
- Exchange Rates
- International Trade and Monetary issues
- Customer Drivers

## • SOCIAL

Trends in social factors of a country or even the world can impact the demand for your products and/or services - and even how your company operates. For example, a population that's skewed towards the older end of the scale may lack an ample supply of younger workers, which would drive up the cost of labor. Also, social attitudes towards businesses and specific industry practices might also affect how your company is accepted in a certain country. Therefore, look closely at the following social elements where you're doing business:

- Rate of Population Growth and Demographic Profile
- Health and Education trends
- Social Mobility and Employment Patterns
- Public Opinions, Attitudes and Taboos
- Lifestyle Choices and Transitions
- Consumer Buying Patterns
- Ethnic and Religious Factors
- Ethical Issues

## • TECHNOLOGY

Technology can bring far-reaching change to how a business operates. We all know how the Internet made international business much easier – and how microchips revolutionized communication and computer technology. Technology can impact cost, quality and innovation, among other critical business factors.

That's why it's crucial not to bury your head in the sand and to be aware of the next wave of technological advances coming your way.

Here are important technological aspects to be aware of:

- Energy Innovations and Mandates
- Internet "Cloud" and IT systems
- Competing Technology Development
- R&D Activity and Funding
- Maturity of Existing Technology
- Technological Impact on Consumer Buying Patterns
- Technology Legislation
- Licensing and Patents

## III. USING THE T.O.W.S. ANALYSIS

The T.O.W.S. analysis is another useful way to gain critical insight into your future business planning, especially if you keep your P.E.S.T. findings in mind. The following diagram will give you a visual map of how the T.O.W.S. analysis (**Threats, Opportunities, Weaknesses, and Strengths**) can be effectively implemented:

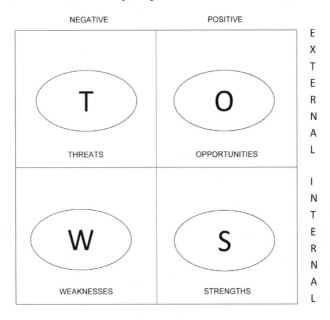

With the T.O.W.S, you should first uncover your external negatives and positives (Threats and Opportunities), so you can view them objectively, without being prejudiced by the awareness of your internal negatives and positives (Weaknesses and Strengths).

Here are some questions to consider when you list these external factors:

- **THREATS**

  - What are your challenges?
  - What are your main competitors doing?
  - What economic changes are occurring that will affect your business?
  - What changes are happening in terms of your customers?
  - Will bad debt or cash flow impede your progress?
  - Which way is market demand heading for your products/services?
  - What other business weaknesses might threaten your profitability?

- **OPPORTUNITIES**

  - What are the best opportunities that your business can take advantage of?
  - What trends can you tap into?
  - What profitable niche markets can you identify?
  - What are the weaknesses of your main competition? How can you exploit those weaknesses?
  - Can you develop any useful strategic partnerships?
  - How can your current business network of contacts help you?
  - Which new markets are worth exploring?
  - What new marketing ideas and strategies can help you expand sales?

Next, consider these questions as you list your internal factors:

- **WEAKNESSES**

  - Where is your business at a disadvantage?
  - What needs improving?

- What are you not doing as well as you should?

- What should you avoid?

- What do your customers perceive to be your weaknesses?

- What knowledge, experience or skills are you in need of?

- Do you have any known vulnerabilities?

- Do you have the necessary management and support capabilities?

• **STRENGTHS**

- What advantages does your business enjoy?

- What do you do well?

- What is unique about your business?

- What resources do you have access to?

- What do your customers perceive to be your strengths?

- What superior knowledge, experience or skills do you possess?

- What do you offer that is distinctive from or superior to your main competition?

- What are your accreditations, qualifications and certifications?

When you've listed all the elements of your T.O.W.S., insert them into the provided grid inserted earlier into this section. This will give you the most crucial overall analysis of where your business currently stands, where you need to improve and what strengths you have to build on.

## IV. GENERATING IDEAS

Now that you've uncovered all relevant information to your business, it's time to begin generating ideas, utilizing this information as your foundation. This should be a three-step process, with the first step, **Brainstorming**. At this phase, you should feel free to put down any and all ideas, even if they may seem ridiculous to you at first; some of the greatest business innovations come from this kind of free-thinking.

The second step, **Thinking It Through**, will be where you begin to filter out the ideas that most obviously will not work for whatever reason; time and money constraints, impracticality, market realities, etc.

Finally, with the **Moving Forward** step, keep in mind that every action causes a reaction. You may be able to pull off the idea - but what impact will it have on your company, your competition and the marketplace?

Use the grid below to put your ideas through this three step process to ensure your ideas for business development are practical, have merit and will positively affect your company's future.

| Brainstorming | Thinking Through | Moving Forward |
|---|---|---|
| *(List every idea you can think of to improve your business - without second-guessing yourself!)* | *(Identify what might stand in the way of implementing your idea – list limitations such as time, cost, market conditions, etc.)* | *(For the remaining viable ideas – what happens if they are actually implemented? How do they impact your business in reality?)* |
| | | |

When you put your business through its paces with the kind of analysis discussed in this chapter, you eliminate obvious pitfalls and you identify your best chances for success. This takes a certain amount of time for the proper research and reflection, but it's time well-spent, as you are concentrating on the most crucial elements that will affect your specific business.

**If you have done your job properly, you will truly find yourself "In It to Win It."**

## ABOUT KIM

As an entrepreneur and business owner with over 40 years of experience, Ong Whatt Kim continues to take an active hands-on role in the overall direction and everyday operation of his group of three companies. Sales are an important part of his business, and Kim believes that entrepreneurs must be excellent salespeople to be successful, and must stay constantly in tune with the ever-changing landscape. Whether or not entrepreneurs are involved in direct selling, a great deal of sales skill is needed to pitch a business plan to potential customers on the business's products or services.

He has a well-rounded training background providing one-on-one coaching as well as conducting public and in-house training and consulting for corporate clients. Kim enjoys imparting his knowledge of the business environment and sharing his practical sales, marketing and management experience. His areas of specialization are in selling, sales management and sales performance coaching.

Ong Whatt Kim is one of the authors featured in Brian Tracy's book, *Counter-Attack*. In his chapter titled, *Know where you are – know where you're going*, Kim shares his insight into how to sustain your business in difficult times.

Ong Whatt Kim is constantly looking for strategic alliances.

For more information, please visit: www.mamsa.com.sg or email him at: whattkim@mamsa.com.sg

CHAPTER 22

# Passion For What I Am Selling

## By Phil Williams

Passion is defined as any powerful or compelling emotion or feeling, as <u>love</u> or hate. Being passionate about what I am selling requires I believe in the product or service, and that I can perform to the best of my ability to make what I do happen. I believe in myself and I have to have an attitude of success and courage. Nothing can stand in my way to stop me from accomplishing what I undertake. I am determined to get the correct information to my client and myself so we can make the correct decision to fill their needs and wants. Whatever I undertake, I will succeed.

I have been asked time and time again, why are you so positive and upbeat? In 2002 I was given an opportunity to enjoy a healthy life. My health had deteriorated and there were a few times that I thought it was not going to get any better. I was on dialysis and had been a diabetic all my life. The diabetes had caused my kidneys to fail. Through the gift of a 19-year-old that was an organ donor, I was given an unbelievable gift. I was the recipient of a kidney and pancreas transplant. A young man had lost his life and donated his organs to me. He had given me the gift of life. Nothing else mattered from that time on. Be thankful and passionate with whatever I undertake, and make sure I treat people with the utmost kindness and respect. There is nothing in what I do or how I do it, that can't have a positive outcome.

I wake up every morning and face another day. What a morning. What an opportunity. As my feet hit the floor a new and exciting day begins. As a sales professional, each day brings new excitement. The reason we all got into this profession is the opportunity to help our clients and our families. There is nothing that will happen that can change my attitude. Problems become opportunities to excel and successes are to be built on as a strong foundation. If something does go wrong, it is usually because we did not have enough information to make the correct decision. And that is up to us. Learn from it and use it to make you stronger.

My expertise is multi-family housing. My passion is to make sure my clients make the best investment and obtain the greatest opportunity for themselves and their families. Many people complain about market conditions, the economy, and all the rest. They get swallowed up in their own self-doubts. The anchor around their neck drags them to the depths of destruction. They look at what is better for themselves rather than what is best for their client. The number one concern for me is my client's success. I succeed because I want to succeed. Any other person or thing does not control my success. It is up to me to find out what my clients needs are and put together the puzzle that makes the opportunity happen. Wow, is this an amazing opportunity?

The most important criteria investors are looking for today are good buildings that are performing at their peak. Assets that are cash flowing. The idea of building equity by sitting and waiting for market conditions to change is a slow growth process. Investors are looking at cash on cash returns. What and how are we going to get this building to perform at its peak? It seems pretty simple, raise rents and cut expenses. Easy solution to a very complex problem. There are two influencing factors in our company's thirty five-year experience that control this. Job growth is directly related to rental income. These are the two key factors. Over the past thirty-five years, as job growth goes up on the positive side of the equation, rents follow. As job growth goes negative, the rental market does the same. We have tracked this and the results are dead on. The rental growth or decline is usually not far behind what the job growth behavior is doing. What an amazing tool to help plan and look at the rental market and performance of a building.

Treat your client just as you would like to be treated. It seems simple, but actually doing it can be very difficult. One of the most important ways to start building a relationship with a client is to take an x-ray of their business, situation or problem. Just as if we went to a cardiologist and you say to him, "Hey Doc, I have a pain in my chest." And he says to get the scalpel and let's start cutting. You say, "Hold on, how about an x-ray or running some tests?" This isn't going to make you feel all warm and fuzzy about his abilities. There are three things that make the difference of being average or great. It starts with the way you listen. The old saying, "The reason you have two ears and one mouth is so you can listen twice as hard." What a great way to help a client. Ask questions to find out what their needs are. Let them complete their thought without interruption. Listen and look for an opportunity to give your solution to their situation. Second, take excellent notes. Ask if it is all right for you to jot a few of the ideas down. Remember, successful people love to tell you their story. And people having trouble do not want to readily admit to failure. While taking notes, mark the opportunities you may help them with. And the third step is to review what they had said, and ask for agreement. "Is there anything else you would like to tell me? Is there anything else we can cover today? Can you think of anything we might have left out?" Questions, these give you an opportunity to know how or why your client does business the way they do.

What do we do with this information? We have shown our client we are truly interested in what they have to say and what their concerns might be. At that point is up to us to come up with a solution to what they want or what they need. Something I do is treat the opportunity or property as if it were my own – with the same excitement and enthusiasm I portray every day. I believe you have to care about your clients needs as if they were your own. Take ownership of them. For me, it gives me more drive and tenacity for the project at hand. In future contacts with this person, we have some common ground to start our discussion. Make sure we have taken notes about personal matters, trips, and new purchases and ask how that particular item might be doing. This shows concern, interest and knowledge about your client. Once we are done with the discussion, it is time to get to the meat of our contact. What have we found? Where are we? Does this offer the solution we were both looking for?

I have a story about a client of mine. She had just lost her husband and had just been fitted for a walker. I had called her back a few weeks after I had talked with her and asked if she was doing ok after she lost her husband? She told me all was fine. And I asked her how she was doing with her new walker? And she was very surprised I had asked her about that. We talked a little more and she looks forward to my monthly call to check in on her and see how her apartment building is performing. I have answered questions for her about her building while consistently strengthening the business relationship we have. I am saying to take the information you receive, store it however you may in today's world and use it to show your clients you know and understand their needs and you are available to help them. *Doing the little extra is what makes the difference.*

We all want to be the best we can be. ...Accomplish the most we can. ...Be as successful as possible. There is only one thing that holds us back from being what we want. It is us. We must take responsibility for what we do, how we perceive things and what the results are. There is an old saying, "If it's to be, it's up to me." Be very thankful for whatever situation you find yourself in. Successful or not, you have the opportunity to do more and work harder. Take on the larger projects and know you will succeed and overcome whatever roadblock may be in your way. We look at the most successful people and try to do or copy what they do. To a point, that might be fine. What I have found is we all have our own strengths and weaknesses. The idea is to play to your strengths. I believe that is very important to be successful. You know what you are good at, so become great using those assets. Learn to improve on you weaknesses and whatever you are trying to accomplish will be easier to obtain.

A trait I have taken very seriously is following through – making sure what I say I am going to do. No matter what the results may be, I must complete what I have promised. I have found it is so important in building a relationship with a client; it must be part of your work ethic. I just don't go through the motions, I take the opportunity on as if it is the most important thing I have ever done. If it is important enough for your client to ask me to do it, then it is that important for me to complete the task. *When someone asks us to do something or we volunteer to do something for someone, we have to follow through.*

Respecting client's wants or needs may be trivial with respect to what the larger picture is. But doing those requests with diligence and enthusiasm is what builds a solid relationship with your client. When your client thinks about whatever you are selling or producing, you want them to think of you as the very best in your field. When you say you are going to do or accomplish something, it gets done. This builds the relationship of trust and integrity. We are only as good as our word. It is amazing, do one good thing for a client and they might tell a few people. Do something wrong with that same client, and you may never recover from the mistake. We have to be very aware of what we can or can't deliver.

Finally, putting this all together. I have had many mentors in my career. I have seen how they became successful. I have taken their habits and adopted them to my own strengths.

You have to believe in what you are doing. It is the most important thing you do every day for yourself, your family and your clients. Your success depends on you. As the hours of the day move on and we stop performing at our capacity, those minutes, those hours ...are lost forever. We have to make the most of the time we have. Whether it is with our families, our clients, or ourselves, that time is very valuable to all of us. Throughout our lives we have people cross our paths and leave us with little nuggets of knowledge and advice. *It is up to us to take those nuggets and turn them into gold and have the passion to share with others.*

## About Phil

Phil Williams puts to work his forty years of experience in customer service and sales every day at PCLC, Inc., a boutique brokerage specializing in apartment buildings sales in the San Francisco Bay Area. Utilizing his extensive background in managing and leading large-scale sales operations, Phil also spearheaded PCLC's call center strategy.

Born and raised in San Leandro, Phil's family has owned apartment buildings in the area for over four generations, dating back to the early settling of the East Bay. Over the years, Phil has become an expert on the history and unique facets of this city as well as its neighboring municipalities.

Phil attended Chabot Junior College, the College of San Mateo, and California State College at Hayward and is a licensed Real Estate Agent. He is also president of the Homeowners Association, a member of the California State Horsemen's Association Scholarship Committee and the USGA, and also acts as an Ambassador for the California Transplant Donor Network, which involves speaking to groups and educating them on organ donations. In addition, Phil is dedicated to his role as a member of the San Leandro Boys and Girls Club Board of Directors, which encourages young people to graduate from high school, become model citizens and give back to the community.

Phil describes himself as being "in a world of women," as he and his wife have three daughters and two granddaughters. The couple also has two adopted dogs, both Cavalier King Charles Spaniels. Horseback riding, golf and reading are some of Phil's favorite pastimes.

# CHAPTER 23

# Success: A Game Of Inches

## By Lance Gordon

After watching the Wisconsin Badgers football team win the historic first Big Ten Championship in Indianapolis, I remember hearing the insightful comment made by Mark Dantonio, the Michigan State coach. After all the analytical comments were aired, he boiled the entire loss down to one significant factor. He said, "It's a game of inches."

Jeff Olson, in his book, *The Slight Edge*, comments that the difference between champions and the "rest of the pack" is not that the champions do monumental feats that everyone else fails to do. Rather, they consistently do the little things over and over again, on a regular basis. The difference between first and second place prize money is huge in horse racing. The distance between the winner and second place loser may be a few inches – "Won by a nose," as the cliché goes.

I have found that Dantonio's game of inches comment applies to two related concepts. First, you have the six inches between your ears – the power of your attitude. Second, there's Jeff Olson's Slight Edge philosophy – the little extras you do on a consistent basis each day that make a huge difference over an extended period of time. Your mental attitude will determine how consistently and diligently you perform those little extra activities, the behavior that sets you apart from the average person.

In my book, *Building the Ultimate Network*, I mentioned that the Law of Large Numbers would usually offset anyone's lack of talent. By relentlessly engaging in massive action, you could overcome almost any shortcomings.

In the early stage of my sales career, I discovered some audio tapes from a brilliant trainer named Tom Hopkins. I traveled for business every day, so I listened to the tapes in my car. In Tom's words, "my car became a university on wheels." Instead of listening to music on the radio, I received professional development training.

The tapes taught me valuable sales techniques, but there was more. Unbeknownst to me, my attitude was shifting. I first became aware of this attitude adjustment when I worked as a government employee. As my attitude changed, I became aware of the negative atmosphere at work. Many of the people I worked with had little ambition; their goal was to make it to Friday. I began to develop an intolerance for negative people and I stayed away from the office as much as possible.

Little did I know, I was starting to apply the "game of inches" to my attitude. It formed a newfound confidence. For me, failure was not an option. If I felt strongly enough about a project, I prepared for only one outcome: Success. I was always "in it to win it," so when I heard the title of this book, I knew I had to share my story.

My crisis while working for the government led me to seek a change in my life. With a family to support, I decided to start my own home-based business while keeping my job. I started selling insurance and, in two years, began earning more part time than at my full-time job.

In 1996, one of my clients educated me on the fortunes being made on the deregulation of the telecommunications industry. Companies like MCI and Sprint could now compete with AT&T. I finally found what I had been searching for. I dreamed big and set ambitious goals – including those little extras I would do each day. I was *in it to win it* and enjoyed eight years of immense success. During those eight years, I was fortunate enough to work with a man by the name of Steve Schulz, who has been mentioned in many books as one of the greatest sales trainers in the history of the direct selling industry. His influence cast a winning attitude that has helped me survive the roller coaster cycles we all encounter.

Ultimately, deregulation invited incredible competition and eroding profit margins. Due to circumstances beyond my control, the company had failed. Not me, the company. Now I needed a new opportunity to apply the invaluable lessons I had learned over the previous years.

Over time, I became involved in several business ventures with moderate success. Then, in March of 2009, I discovered Javalution, a Florida company that had developed a vitamin-fortified coffee called JavaFit. I loved the concept, and the people at the company impressed me. They had the same attitude I had always embraced. These guys had been hit with every obstacle and nothing had stopped them – not even the worst hurricane in Florida history that destroyed their Miami headquarters.

I soon developed a strong relationship with Javalution's president. A former Wall Street whiz, he too followed his dream of owning his own company. The company saw problems as challenges. The law of attraction was working – I could follow an organization with that attitude. The company's goal was to make Javalution a publicly-traded company. They believed they could do it within a year. I thought this was unrealistic, but it didn't matter. I was committed to follow this company to its ultimate success. To my surprise, Javalution went public in 2010 under the symbol JCOF. In January of 2011, it traded at 9 cents per share. By June, it had hit $ 2.08 – more than a 2300 percent gain!

The company had not only caught my eye, but the attention of some major players in direct selling. Richmont Holdings founder John Rochon was impressed with the product and the vision of the company, and he formed a strategic alliance with the company in 2010. John Rochon is always *in it to win it* and that attitude has brought him uncanny success. The strategic alliance with Javalution and his company helped initiate a series of mergers and acquisitions that could change the face of the direct selling industry.

Javaluation soon merged with Youngevity, a California-based health company founded by Dr. Joel Wallach. Within weeks, Financial Destination Inc. merged with Youngevity. Several smaller companies also came under the umbrella of companies that would later become A.L. International, with offices all over the United States and the world. As of this writing, the company is positioned for global expansion and billion-dollar growth.

Now, you might be thinking that all you have to do is dream big and have ambitious goals to receive whatever you want out of life. Some "systems" imply this, but dreaming and ambition are just part of the formula. Most success is achieved as the result of significant effort over a long period of time – and it helps to have a winning attitude backed by persistence to overcome every obstacle.

If anyone can do it, why aren't more people successful?

Consider my own story: Fast success in the insurance business, virtually immediate success in telecommunications, connecting with a startup coffee company and "falling into" the beginning of a future billion-dollar company. Life's been pretty simple for me, right?

In reality, no. When I started in insurance, I didn't sell a single policy for six months. The first people I talked to about changing their telephone carrier thought I was crazy to compete with AT&T. Just about everyone drinks coffee, but even that business presented challenges that pushed my winning attitude to the limit. In each business, I reached a point where I had to consider giving up. The six inches between my ears gave me two choices. I could either make money or I could make excuses. But I realized I could not make both.

I watched many distributors in both the telecom and coffee businesses quit without ever making any money. Others experienced success. What separated the quitters from those who stayed to see the job through? A book published during the great depression may provide a clue.

Napoleon Hill's *Think and Grow Rich* has remained on best seller lists more than 70 years since it was first published. Hill spent years interviewing some of this country's most successful men. His goal was to find a common thread that made them all massively successful, the one thing that separated them from the rest of the pack. The book contains 16 Laws of Success, but just one pervasive theme: a successful man or woman avoids people who attempt to dissuade them from their goals.

Imagine what Alexander Graham Bell's peers said when they heard that he was going to talk through a wire. What did Thomas Edison's friends and family say when he set out to invent the light bulb? What kind of reception do you think Sam Walton got when he boasted that he was going to become bigger than Sears & Roebuck?

Your dream may be smaller than theirs. But whatever your dream, make it big by your own standards. Set your goals, then have the mindset to make them a reality. Here's the tough part. People will try to persuade you to quit, they will laugh at your goals, and they will do everything in their power to make you fail. Some are casual acquaintances or friends. Others are closer than that. You might even be married to one of them.

Negative people pose the greatest threat to your success. Most often, they either think your success draws attention to their own failures, or they believe they are protecting you from disappointment.

*Orlando Sentinel* columnist Bo Poertner coined the term "CAVE people" in 1990, and while he was referring to citizens who opposed a new ordinance, I find it applies to the people who want you to fail. CAVE stands for Citizens Against Virtually Everything.

Believe me when I say, being successful is simple but not easy. First, you must only spend time with positive, self-motivated individuals. Second, you have to develop a powerful mental attitude that keeps you from quitting and repels the negativity that surrounds you. Third, you have to reinforce your positive thinking on a daily basis.

If you have friends who are not success-motivated, or they bring negativity into your life, you have two choices. You can change their attitude or find new friends. As your own positive mindset develops, you will find it uncomfortable to associate with negative people. They are as repelled by your positive thinking as you are by their negative thinking. Often, they are relatives, so contact with them may be required at family events.

The issue is incredibly more complex if it is your spouse. Unless you are considering divorce, you must deal with this negativity. A spouse is much more supportive if the business venture becomes profitable. When I was selling insurance part time, I won several exotic trips. I encouraged my wife to join me, and she became much more supportive. Before starting my last venture, I registered the business in my wife's name so she could have a sense of ownership. The improvement in her attitude and support really made a huge difference.

Your powerful mental attitude must do more than withstand outside negative influences. It also has to be strong enough to counter your own negative thoughts. Evangelical Christian pastor and author Charles Swindoll says that, "Life is 10% what happens to you and 90% how you react to it."

One of my favorite, inspiring movies is *Cinderella Man,* starring Russell Crowe. In one scene, where underdog Jim Braddock appears unable to stand up to the much stronger Art Lasky's punching power, Braddock's manager tells him to "beat him from the inside out." He meant that if Braddock destroyed Laskys' internal (mental) attitude, the six inches between his ears, he would beat his superior outside physical strength. It worked and resulted in the upset of the decade.

Mental attitude is big business. Hundreds of thousands of individuals consume self-development material – books, recordings, seminars given by top speakers. Merely being exposed to this material is meaningless unless you are committed to applying it to your daily activities.

You must do it daily. It can be brief. Fifteen minutes to half an hour are sufficient. Read a motivational or professional book. Listen to CD's in your car, on your computer or on your home entertainment system. Conversely, limit your exposure to newspapers or negative news stations. They fill your mind with negative thoughts.

When Javalution merged with Youngevity, I met a man named Tom Chenault, one of their top distributors and a legend in the direct selling industry. He developed his own radio show and has motivated thousands of people over the years. Each weekday morning at 7:30 a.m. Central Time, Tom hosts a "Hair on Fire" phone call that lasts just ten minutes, enough to pump self- motivational thoughts into his sales team all over the country. The first time I listened to the call, I heard Tom use two slogans I've used for years to motivate myself every day. He said he was *in it to win it* and that he "does not work part time, he does not work full time, he works all the time." I make the time for that daily call, and I encourage my sales team to do the same.

Imagine being surrounded by positive, self-motivated people who are not impacted by negativity and are not afraid of rejection. That would be nice, but the problem is, most of them are probably under the age of five. By the time they get to school and are tested for placement, or they experience peer pressure, or negativity, or competition, or confrontation, they begin to lose their confidence. We are all born winners. Somewhere along the way, many of us lose that winning attitude. Winston Churchill said that "attitude is a small thing that makes a big difference."

Success is a game of inches, not feet or yards. How you develop and coach those precious six inches between your ears can give you the slight edge you need to reach success you never thought possible.

## About Lance

Lance Gordon was the number one money earner and Affiliate of the Year with JavFit Healthy Coffee before its merger with Youngevity Life Sciences out of Chula Vista, California. He quickly rose to Senior Executive Marketing Director with the merged company called FDI-Youngevity. His meteoric rise to success in network marketing dates back to 1996 with a Billion Dollar NYSE company called Excel Communication Inc., where he catapulted to the highest level and a six digit income in his first year. He landed on the Top Performers Council, earned a Top Ten Diamond Award, and became a Circle of Excellence winner over an eight-year career – before building large organizations with three other companies.

Lance's sales career started even earlier. At American United Life, the young rep received the New Agents Performance Award which was given to the top new agent in the company. He later helped launch a new physician-owned company in Wisconsin and made the President's Club his first five years with the company. He has used his marketing skills to found and grow LGA Tax Services LLC into one of the largest privately-owned tax businesses in Milwaukee.

A faculty member at the University of Phoenix, Lance teaches accounting and finance courses in the undergraduate and MBA programs. He was an instructor for the Becker CPA Review Course, a national training director with Excel Communications, and trained on stage at the Excel National Conventions in Dallas, Texas. Lance has written several tax articles and co-authored *Building The Ultimate Network,* which has made at least two best seller lists. He received the National Academy of Best Selling Authors award in 2011.

Lance received his BA in Business Administration and Marketing from Wartburg College in Waverly, Iowa, earned a Masters Degree in tax law from the University of Wisconsin-Milwaukee, and a Masters in Information Systems from North Texas State University.

Lance enjoyed competitive football in high school and at the college level and is part owner of an NFL football team.

You can connect with Lance at lancegordon@att.net

# CHAPTER 24

# Becoming a Purpose-Driven Entrepreneur! – Building a Business with No Expiration Date!

## By Bart Queen

This is not for the AVERAGE businessperson.

For the majority of business people, THIS WILL NOT EVEN MAKE SENSE.

IF YOU THINK BEING IN BUSINESS IS ABOUT YOU AND WHAT YOU CAN GET, ...STOP READING NOW, AND GO READ SOMEONE ELSE'S CHAPTER!

This is for those who want to be MORE…who want to become a person of total influence…WHO WANT TO DO MORE…who want to leave a legacy of hope, difference and inspiration for others AND FOR THOSE WHO WANT TO GIVE MORE — those who want to develop a mindset of "**GIVINNOVATION!**"

If that is you…answer the following questions…your success, your future business life, your future personal success and your legacy lies in the answers to the next six questions.

Questions to ask:

1. Are you doing what you love?

2. Have you mastered your message to the point of a skillful art? Have you turned the art of communication into the science of results?

3. Do you want to make a dent in the universe?

4. Are you selling dreams or products?

5. Are you creating insanely great experiences for your customers?

6. Do you believe and live out the premise that your whole purpose is to make the lives of your customers better? ...PERIOD!

If you answered NO to even one of those questions...keep reading!

These six questions are the foundation for the success of Steve Jobs and Apple. They created the mindset that allows anyone to move from a businessman with a "job" to a PURPOSE-DRIVEN ENTREPRENEUR, from a business that has an unsure future to a business with NO SHELF LIFE and NO EXPIRATION DATE!

I truly believe we are living in the best time to start, build and grow a business. The factors have never been more difficult in the eyes of your average entrepreneur. The reality is ...the opportunity has never been more open, the gap never greater, the void never emptier, the timing never more perfect! All you need to do is SEE the opportunity, STAND in the gap, FILL the void, and HAVE THE COURAGE to start! There has only been one other opportunity almost as great as the one we have right now, ...THE GREAT DEPRESSION! The Great Depression produced more millionaires than any other time in history! I believe we are positioned to produce more billionaires than ever before. That thought is only for those who dare to approach business from a different philosophy. That thought is only for those who dare to redefine innovation; that thought is only for those who DARE to live out their purpose!

It doesn't matter if you are just starting your business, been in business a short time, or you have a successful business, ...NOW IS THE TIME TO ACT!

Sometimes as I speak to men and women about their businesses, they give me a funny look when I talk about their business 'strategy' and not their business 'plan.' I ask, "Does your business have an expiration date?" They come back quickly with the response, "Of course not!" I then ask, "How are you planning for your business to extend long after your personal date has expired?"

I don't believe these people have ever thought about being a purpose-driven entrepreneur or creating a business with no shelf life.

USA today has an article on Bill Cosby with the headline …"Bill Cosby Prides Himself on Comedy that has No Shelf Life." The entire article is about how timeless his comedy is!

What are things that come to mind when you hear the term, "No Shelf Life"? Here are some examples of no shelf life and must be used immediately:

1. Coconuts. Young coconuts are perishable. They virtually have no shelf life.

2. Cask ale has no shelf life and is highly perishable.

3. Expensive caviar has no shelf life.

On the other side, items that have no shelf life and can be used indefinitely include:

1. Real black gunpowder has no shelf life – if stored properly!

2. Rechargeable flashlight batteries – if re-charged correctly have no shelf life!

3. Distilled spirits – an unopened bottle has no shelf life.

"Shelf life" from Wikipedia is defined as the length of time that foods, beverages chemicals and many other perishable items are given before they are considered unsuitable for sale, use or consumption.

There are a few differences to think about:

**"Shelf life"** has to do with quality. **"Expiration date"** has to with safety. **"Service life"** has to do with the expected lifetime or the acceptable period of use in service.

The United States Department of Defense (DoD) Shelf-Life Program defines shelf-life as: The total period of time beginning with the date of manufacture, date of cure (for elastomeric and rubber products only), date of assembly, or date of pack (subsistence only), and terminated by the date by which an item must be used (expiration date) or subjected to inspection, test, restoration, or disposal action; or after inspection/laboratory test/restorative action that an item may remain in the combined wholesale (including manufacturer's) and retail storage systems and still be suitable for issue or use by the end user. Shelf life is not to be confused with service-life. (Service-life is defined as: A general term used to quantify the average or standard life expectancy of an item or equipment while in use. When a shelf-life item is unpacked and introduced to mission requirements, installed into intended application, or merely left in storage, placed in pre-expended bins, or held as bench stock, shelf-life management stops and service life begins.)[11]

The questions we face are two fold as purpose-driven entrepreneurs!

1. How do we create businesses that have no shelf life?
2. How do we develop products that create a service life that becomes a legacy?

I call this the LIFE TIME SERVICE MANAGEMENT MODEL. **[insert graphic?]** This model has allowed me to build my business from no customers to over 500K in year one. It can help you do the same and more! The model has three components: customer acquisition strategies, customer retention strategies and core story. If you have been a part of any marketing experience you will recognize these terms. What is different is the simplicity of how I look at these and how I approach them. The concepts themselves are not rocket science................the application is!

Let's build the mindset first! The foundation to make this model work is critical. Most people are not willing to make the investment of time and effort. I have spent from hours to days helping entrepreneurs to develop and get this part right. The rest of the model is easy once the foundation is in place.

1. Make sure your vision and purpose is crystal clear. This will come out of the process of developing your core story. This is also the foundation for your unique brand. This alone set you

apart from everyone else. Steve Jobs said passion is the fuel for the rocket, but vision directs the rocket. I so remember when he spoke to the gentleman at Coca Cola, "Do you want to sell sugar water or change the world?" We know how the story went, ...can you articulate YOUR vision in less than 10 seconds?

I am committed to giving one million people their voice. To one million people living out their life purpose, to one million people changing the lives of one million more.

2. Are you truly committed to the core concept as PURPOSE-DRIVEN ENTREPRENEURS? Our job is to make the lives of our customers better. The best way to do that is to share what you have learned and comfort those with the comfort you have been comforted with. *What you have learned in the dark share in the light!*

3. Become a strategic communicator at all three levels – content, delivery and interaction. Jobs mastered his message. This is not optional!

Have you mastered your message?

Master the key concepts in customer acquisition and customer retention:

(i)   - build trust.

(ii)  - build relationship.

(iii) - build engagement.

These concepts are what make up the LIFETIME SERVICE MODEL.

(i). Everything you do should drive to one of these goals. In the book, "God is a Sales Person", author Mark Steven's makes the comment, "People buy trust before they buy a solution, tool or product!" Think about people you do business with. You have a mechanic, barber, hairdresser, dry cleaner, plumber, doctor, re-altor or car dealership that you only do business with! You trust them. I raise Clydesdale horses as a hobby. Several years ago, I wanted to buy a wagon for the horses and found one on the Internet in Canada. I spoke with the gentleman for 45 minutes. We had a tremendous conversation. I bought the wagon. I sent the man a check because I trusted him. The day my wagon arrived from Canada to my home in North Carolina he called me. He built trust and relationship! Our number one goal every day should be to build trust with our family, friends and customers!

(ii). Build relationship - people do business with people they like! Your question is how do I build the LIKE-ABILITY FACTOR? Your core story builds the like-ability factor! This links to the second level of my selling model, ME TOO!! Think about those times when you met someone, had a brief conversation, walked away and said, "WOW! I am just like them or we have so much in common." Certain fraternities create this, the Marines, attending the same school, having a similar experience like cancer, or families with special needs. These things create automatic relationships and ME TOO factors!

Remember "people want to be a part of something bigger than themselves." We all have a natural place, fit, or connection to give back. One of my favorite old pieces of wisdom is "comfort those with the comfort you have been comforted with!" Much like today, businesses want to do business with companies that have a green initiative. This is the same principle. People want to do business with people with whom they share a common experience, concern or philosophy. One of my clients does a huge amount of work in education. My commitment to reaching youth, to give them the belief of following their vocation, makes for a solid partnership. One of my recent clients was involved in the Big Brother Big Sister program. This again made a perfect link with my youth program. Today we are doing business together! The result – high likeability factors on both sides, being a part of something bigger than ourselves, high engagement factors and a lot of "ME TOO."

(iii). Build engagement! Engagement is the ability to get the listener, customer, guest, client, student, and prospect to listen, respond and interact! This should be done through our face-to-face meeting, over the phone, and web presence.

If our customers are engaged, they should be saying, "Tell me more!" They should not be saying, "Is it over yet?"

## CUSTOMER BUILDING STRATEGIES
## CUSTOMER RETENTION STRATEGIES
## YOUR CORE STORY

The situation today for most individuals, entrepreneurs and business owners is how do they separate themselves from the pack? How do I gain the continuous edge in everything I do?

Most business owners will race out to buy the newest piece of technology, fancy process or system. Some will invest thousands of dollars in the shiny new thing believing it will give them the new edge. They keep missing the most powerful tool and concept which they have at their fingertips.

I have seen large corporations send their sales people through fancy training courses to learn new strategies for gaining customers. Most employees look at it as the flavor of the month. They never embrace the training. It eventually falls to the wayside. They go back to doing exactly what they have always done. The end result is getting the same thing they have always GOT!!! Sales people have a natural way of doing their selling. We never teach them how to tap into it. We force them into processes and systems that don't allow their authenticity to come forward! We don't teach them how to leverage their most powerful tool in every interaction and selling situation. This is a global condition. This is not a local problem!

The complication is that entrepreneurs, business owners and VP's of sales organizations are missing the mark with their customers. Cost of sales keeps going higher, customer loyalty becomes an abstract idea and customer service becomes a process – not a reach-out personal relationship.

Business becomes TRANSACTION BASED, NOT RELATIONSHIP BASED!

Business becomes PROCESS BASED, NOT AN ONGOING EXPERIENCE!

Business becomes a ONE WAY FLOW, NOT A MUTUAL EXCHANGE OF SERVICES!

Business becomes a CONSTANT HUNT AND CONQUER, NOT A DEVELOPMENT AND NUTURE FOCUS!

The question then becomes how do I separate myself from the pack of the masses? How do I win the race in business not once, not twice, but every time? How do I create the experience where people seek me out? How do I become the magnet people want to do business with? How do I create a relationship with people that exceeds loyalty?

HOW DO I BECOME THE GURU OF MY TOPIC, AREA, BUSINESS AND NICHE?

I believe your core story is your competitive differentiator. Your core story creates the uniqueness that only you have. Your core story gives you the competitive advantage that no one else has...IT SETS YOU APART FROM EVERYONE ELSE! Your core story allows for authenticity. Your core story is your secret weapon!!!

Through this chapter I want you to do two things as you read: one, become aware of the benefits of a core story. Two, begin to visualize using your core story in every aspect of your business!

Here is what I know you will find: you will find you can approach your business from a total different perspective, "a purpose-driven" perspective. You will find you have uncovered an untapped natural market that demands only you. You become the magnet. You will find people seek you out; referrals become a marketing machine on steroids! Most importantly your uniqueness and authenticity is your competitive differentiator! GURU STATUS IS ACHIEVED!!!

In this chapter, I will cover the concept of people buy from people, the mindset shift of empowering others but not impressing others, and the three levels of selling.

correct order is: one – sell yourself, two – sell your solution, tool or product and, third – sell your company.

The second is "ME TOO". There are thousands of ways to create the ME TOO factor. One important way is to share some type of vulnerability or painful experience. I do not mean share your therapy. I mean share what you have learned!!! This allows you to be real. The result is higher trust, stronger like-ability factor and people saying ME TOO!

Now the final level, "I NEED YOU!" This is what we all strive for! This is where all our concepts and ideas come together as one!

Trust is high!

Relationship is high!

Engagement is high!

Like-ability factor is high!

Empowerment is high!

ME TOO factor is high!

The result is "I want what you have! I NEED YOU!"

The strongest results of developing and sharing your core story are threefold! You reach a market that you didn't even know existed, your core story does not have a shelf life. Your uniqueness is your key differentiator! People buy from people. People buy from people they like. People buy from you!

Your core story is your unique differentiator! Everything that has happened to you so far, both the good and the difficult, allows you to connect in a unique way. I see the power every day with folks I work with. They discover a purpose-driven approach. They realize a laser focus. They become the magnet!!! People search them out! I believe you can have this too!!! I believe your core story will make the biggest difference in your business.

My challenge to you is twofold! Look at any successful business or successful businessperson today and find the elements I have described in some way. Look at the people you do business with everyday and identify the concepts that make up a core story. Whether it is in politics, religion, Corporate America, small-to-medium business or the individual owner, you will find the core story.

My challenge to you: If any of these ideas are important to you, email me at bart@speakamerica.com and put in the subject line WIN – CORE STORY. I will be happy to send you details about developing your core story!

The life service model has three key components to customer acquisition and customer retention: build trust, relationship and engagement.

Will you take your business to the NEXT LEVEL?

Here is what I have found in my twenty-three years of helping people communicate their messages. Three principles drive my discussion on your core story. This is the foundation information to build your core story.

1. Understand the concept of people buy from people; people buy from people they like!

2. Work from an approach of EMPOWERING OTHERS! People do not care what you know. This is working from a mindset of IMPRESSING. They care about how much you care and what you have learned. No one can argue with what you have learned through your experience. Develop the philosophy of share and service not sell! This creates an experience of trust, and relationship! The end result is you become a *Trusted Resource*!!

3. Become aware of the three levels of communicating and selling your business.
   a. "SO WHAT"
   b. "ME TOO"   and
   c. "I NEED YOU!"

Understanding these three levels will revolutionize your approach to examining and doing your business! Lets take a look at each one.

"SO WHAT" – This is the hardest level to sell at. This is where 90% of most people work their business. Selling at this level creates two major hurdles to get over. One, the conversation isn't even in their head. Your basic rule is to always "continue the conversation in their head." Two, we sell in the wrong direction. Most people sell in this order - first the company, second the solution, tool, product and third themselves. If you believe in anything I have said so far, if you grasp the concept of people buy from people, then you realize this order will not work! The correct order is: one – sell yourself, two – sell your solution, tool or product and, third – sell your company.

The second is "ME TOO". There are thousands of ways to create the ME TOO factor. One important way is to share some type of vulnerability or painful experience. I do not mean share your therapy. I mean share what you have learned!!! This allows you to be real. The result is higher trust, stronger like-ability factor and people saying ME TOO!

Now the final level, "I NEED YOU!" This is what we all strive for! This is where all our concepts and ideas come together as one!

Trust is high!

Relationship is high!

Engagement is high!

Like-ability factor is high!

Empowerment is high!

ME TOO factor is high!

The result is "I want what you have! I NEED YOU!"

The strongest results of developing and sharing your core story are threefold! You reach a market that you didn't even know existed, your core story does not have a shelf life. Your uniqueness is your key differentiator! People buy from people. People buy from people they like. People buy from you!

Your core story is your unique differentiator! Everything that has happened to you so far, both the good and the difficult, allows you to connect in a unique way. I see the power every day with folks I work with. They discover a purpose-driven approach. They realize a laser focus. They become the magnet!!! People search them out! I believe you can have this too!!! I believe your core story will make the biggest difference in your business.

My challenge to you is twofold! Look at any successful business or successful businessperson today and find the elements I have described in some way. Look at the people you do business with everyday and identify the concepts that make up a core story. Whether it is in politics, religion, Corporate America, small-to-medium business or the individual owner, you will find the core story.

My challenge to you: If any of these ideas are important to you, email me at bart@speakamerica.com and put in the subject line WIN – CORE STORY. I will be happy to send you details about developing your core story!

The life service model has three key components to customer acquisition and customer retention: build trust, relationship and engagement.

Will you take your business to the NEXT LEVEL?

Will you be committed enough to become a PURPOSE-DRIVEN ENTREPRENEUR?

Will you develop, create and grow a BUSINESS THAT HAS NO SHELF LIFE?

Will you be ONE OF THE FEW WHO PUTS A DENT IN THE UNIVERSE?

Will you be BOLD ENOUGH TO SELL DREAMS AND NOT PRODUCTS?

CAN YOU BE committed enough to live out the principle that our SINGLE MOST IMPORTANT PURPOSE IS TO MAKE A DIFFERENCE IN CUSTOMERS LIVES?

I am asking you to JOIN US in creating a REVOLUTION IN BUSINESS TODAY! Will you join us?

IT STARTS WITH YOU!!!!!!!!!!!!!!!!!!!!

I DARE YOU!

## About Bart

Bart Queen, Remarkability Expert
Speak America, CEO
Ultimate PowerSpeak, CEO
Let Your Life Speak Foundation, Founder

In today's global economic environment it has never been more important to have the competitive advantage. The ability to communicate your message clearly, concisely and powerfully is your "silver bullet." Bart is a highly sought after speaker, communication expert and trainer. He is a valued asset and resource in helping individuals and businesses around the world develop solid communications skills for their professional and personal success.

Bart started his communications training company, ULTIMATE POWERSPEAK, over five years ago. ULTIMATE POWERSPEAK operates across industries and with executives, IT professionals, salespeople and individuals in any capacity who are communicating face-to-face or in the virtual world. The result of his training helps them articulate their message more clearly and with greater impact, results and influence.

Bart and the ULTIMATE POWERSPEAK team truly turn the art of communication into the science of REMARKABLE results. He is now dedicated and expanding his efforts to helping people take their communication to the next level and "Letting their Life Speak." In 2008, Bart's team took the ULTIMATE POWERSPEAK communication skills to Kenya and worked with a women's political caucus group and with junior and seniors in high school. This effort has now lead to the goal of reaching five continents in five years and the launching of the National Youth Speak program in the fall of 2009.

As seen in USA today, Bart founded Speak America based on people's longing to make a difference, yet not knowing how. Speak America inspires, develops and helps people realize that difference! Bart, author of "THE 10 KEYS TO REMARKABILITY" shows others how to create remarkable lives.

Speak America is a national resource organization for remarkability. Speak America is dedicated to helping people create and live lives of "Intentional Legacy." Bart has determined through his years of helping people with their communication skills, that when people find their voice, they find their purpose and gift to the world.

Speak America is dedicated to helping people achieve their full realization of that gift. Speak America helps individuals through three key focus areas - ULTIMATE BUSINESS SPEAK, ULTIMATE LIFE SPEAK AND ULTIMATE YOUTH SPEAK. The result of finding your voice and sharing your gift allows people to find their vocation. Bart believes when you are living out your vocation, then and only then, the result is letting your life speak! Bart's goal is to give one million people their "voice."

When your life speaks, you are on the path to remarkability. The Speak America tagline is ....... "BE REMARKABLE, GIVE ME A PLACE TO STAND AND I CAN MOVE THE WORLD!" Speak America will move the world one voice at a time, one gift at a time, one person at a time!

# CHAPTER 25

# Story-Selling:
# The 7 ways To Make Your
# Brand A Blockbuster

## By Nick Nanton, Esq., J.W. Dicks, Esq., Lindsay Dicks and Greg Rollett

Now more than ever, the energy industry is advertising on television. Only they're not directly selling. They're telling *stories* - about how they're creating jobs, helping third-world countries, inspiring kids studying science and helping America become energy-independent.

They're not telling you to buy more gas. They're telling you why you should *root* for them.

No matter how you feel about the politics or economics of the situation, you have to admit that these ads are effective. Why? Because great stories are the backbone of any brand. They elevate them from being just another business to becoming a captivating narrative that demands an audience. And once that audience is caught up in the tale, they can't help but see what product or service that brand is offering for sale.

At the Dicks + Nanton Celebrity Branding Agency, we call that process "Story-Selling" - and we've seen its success pay off over and over again. By using everything from blogs to books to branded films, we employ Story-Selling to help professionals and entrepreneurs connect with their audience on a human level.

Nobody wants to feel like they're the victim of nonstop marketing, which so often happens in today's society. But because Story-Selling is designed to entertain instead of sell, sell, sell, people are willing to lower their guard and "enjoy the show," just as they would any movie, TV episode or book. Story-Selling opens up your potential market in a way that conventional advertising almost never does.

But how do *you* craft the right story for yourself or your company? What's your "plot" that will hook your audience?

There are a few common narratives that all effective stories share, as detailed by Christopher Booker in his book, "Seven Basic Plots: Why We Tell Stories." These plots hit us all on a primal level and draw us in, because they all speak to the human experience in a profound way.

In this chapter, we're going to reveal what those seven basic plots are - and, more importantly, how they can be applied to specific brands through Story-Selling.

## BASIC PLOT #1: OVERCOMING THE MONSTER

### *What's the Story?*
The "Overcoming the Monster" plotline is pretty simple - the hero discovers something evil threatening his homeland and must go out and conquer it. This covers anything from a knight going out to slay a dragon to James Bond going after Goldfinger.

### *How It's Used*
How does a prince slaying a dragon translate to a branding exercise? It turns out, pretty easily. Let's go back to the oil and gas industry. If you think of foreign oil as an "outside evil" that draws us into wars and subjects us to wild price fluctuations, then you can see how our domestic oil and gas industry becomes the hero when it "slays" this particular dragon by uncovering and recovering more of our own energy resources.

### *How You Can Use It*
There are plenty of "monsters" that today's consumer wants to see destroyed - it's just a matter of tailoring your message to that platform. Maybe you're a lawyer who saw other law firms ripping off clients with

excessive fees (the "monster") - and you built your firm differently. Or you're a financial advisor who saw what the crash of 2008 (another "monster") did to innocent people - and you set out to build an investment strategy that safeguards against that happening. There are many ways to go with this plotline that will pay off for any business.

## BASIC PLOT #2: RAGS TO RICHES

### *What's the Story?*

In the late 19th century, the American writer Horatio Alger made a career out of this plot, with a series of novels about young boys born into poverty and achieving amazing success. It's still a hugely popular storyline in this country, if not THE most popular. Such modern folk heroes as Oprah Winfrey and Steve Jobs remain a source of fascination precisely because of their journey from humble roots. Think of the blockbuster "Pretty Woman," starring Julia Roberts, as the ultimate rags-to-riches movie.

### *How It's Used*

How many politicians have you seen advertise their ascent from humble beginnings? Former presidents Ronald Reagan and Bill Clinton certainly did. More importantly, this storyline just did wonders for one of our clients, Tracy Myers, and his car dealership in North Carolina. We produced a branded film for Tracy entitled "Car Men," that ended up getting a red carpet premiere at a local theatre, was played constantly (and for free) on the local TV affiliates (one of which used it as a lead-in to the Super Bowl!), and was even sold as a DVD release. The amount of goodwill and attention "Car Men" generated for Tracy and his business was truly breathtaking.

### *How You Can Use It*

Most of us also built our businesses from nothing or almost nothing - and that story is incredibly relatable to the general public and, most likely, to your specific market. Just sharing how you battled the odds to build a successful business (the plot of "Car Men") makes for a great branded film or book.

## BASIC PLOT #3: THE QUEST

### *What's the Story?*

In The Quest, the hero must leave everyday life behind and go out and seek an object, person, location or just some information that's vital to his or his community's future. "The Lord of the Rings" trilogy and the Indiana Jones movies both exemplify this time-honored storyline.

### *How It's Used*

One of the most groundbreaking ad campaigns in history actually employed The Quest motif - so successfully that it's been going strong for almost forty years. It's "The Pepsi Challenge," in which Pepsi conducts blind taste tests against its competitors at various locations. Pepsi goes directly to the consumers with these taste tests (The Quest) to get vital information about people who prefer Pepsi (the object of The Quest).

### *How You Can Use It*

Did you undergo a quest to find something unique and special to add to your business? We know personal development experts, for example, who promote the fact that they traveled the world to discover the most innovative and effective meditation techniques. If you had to search for the perfect location or the most powerful product or service to sell, that could be your version of The Quest. Understanding what you went through to find what is most vital about what you do also gives an appreciation of that process, as well as an appreciation of your business. That creates a desire in consumers to *buy* this wonderful "something."

## BASIC PLOT #4: THE VOYAGE

### *What's the Story?*

We're off to see the Wizard! In "The Voyage," the hero finds himself sent to a magical place, where everyday rules are no longer in play. At first, the trip is fun until something dark makes itself known, which the hero must conquer. In the process, he or she overcomes some internal problem, and then returns home. A prime example of this plot, as you might have guessed from our intro line, is "The Wizard of Oz," as well as "Gulliver's Travels" and even the children's classic, "Where the Wild Things Are." More modern examples would be "Inception" and, believe it or not, "The Devil Wears Prada."

### *How It's Used*

It's rare to see a conventional business use this storyline in their own personal branding. More common is a company taking the *viewer* of a commercial or the reader of an ad on the voyage - showing them how their product or service can transport them to a "magical land." Think about car commercials where the driver of the advertised vehicle is taken to an imaginary road with awesome vistas or even amazing special effects, or a food item that takes the person who eats it to an animated blissful state.

### *How You Can Use It*

If you're an entrepreneur who has multiple companies, there is an impactful way you can use this storyline. Let's say when you began one of these businesses, you really didn't know what you were doing. You had no experience and suddenly found yourself in an entirely unfamiliar field with its own set of rules of which you were completely ignorant. Nevertheless, you succeeded and "beat the odds." That's basically the voyage - and we know plenty of entrepreneurs who have made it. It's relatable to an audience when they see how little you knew - and how impressive you've become!

## BASIC PLOT #5: COMEDY

### *What's the Story?*

We've all seen enough comedies to know they're usually about situations that are...well, funny; big misunderstandings or people out of their element trying to pull something off they shouldn't try to attempt or pretending to be something they're not. Think of Woody Allen in his early films faking it as a ladies' man, or, more recently, Will Ferrell being the buffoon in any number of scenarios (half of an ice skating team in "Blades of Glory," the manager of a basketball team in "Semi-Pro," an egotistical newscaster in "Anchorman," etc.).

### *How It's Used*

Comedy is a very popular way of Story-Selling when it comes to commercial advertising. Think about it - these days, the Super Bowl is just as famous for its funny ads as it is for the football! For branding purposes, however, it can be tricky business. Obviously, for a Conan O'Brien or Stephen Colbert, comedy is what their brand is all about - the joke is supposed to be on them. For a business leader like Bill Gates or Richard

233

Branson, however, becoming the punch line can be fatal to their credibility. Still, Donald Trump survived being the butt of plenty of insults at a Comedy Central Roast - but his brand has that kind of outrageousness built into it.

### *How You Can Use It*

Again, comedy can be a perilous path to cross. While it's true you want to be entertaining, you still need to maintain your credibility and project your expertise. Still, a small dose of unexpected comedy can sometimes help to close the distance between you and your audience. One of our clients, Darrin Mish, is a tax lawyer who has done numerous videos explaining numerous legal situations with the IRS. In the middle of doing one of these videos, he accidentally knocked the microphone off the desk. Instead of stopping and redoing the entire video, he merely yelled "Oops," picked up the mike from the floor, placed it back on the desk and kept going. To this day, it's one of his most memorable marketing moments - and it helped potential clients relate to him as a person, instead of just another stuffy attorney.

## BASIC PLOT #6: TRAGEDY

### *What's the Story?*

Tragedy, of course, is the other side of comedy - it's all about the *un*happy ending and involves very bad things happening to the protagonist. Shakespeare was big on tragedy - "Romeo and Juliet," "Hamlet" and Macbeth" are all plays where pretty much everybody we like dies. These days, movies like "Scarface" and "Goodfellas" serve as our modern-day tragedies. The "heroes" are, from the beginning, headed towards their doom - and nothing is going to get in the way of that ultimate fate.

### *How It's Used*

Tragedy, like comedy, isn't a real popular branding technique, for obvious reasons! It does tend to work for celebrities who have had substance abuse problems or any other personal problem that takes them from superstar to has-been in record time (think Charlie Sheen). When they go on the cover of "People" magazine with their mea culpa, they gain public sympathy from their private tragedies - and often have a shot at restoring their careers as well. As of this writing, even Charlie Sheen is about to be back on TV with a new sitcom, "Anger Management," after making the media rounds apologizing for his past out-of-control antics.

### *How You Can Use It*

Everybody goes through bad experiences - most of us, of course, would prefer to forget about them and move on. This can be a big mistake, however, because talking about your "tragedies" again makes you relatable to the audience and showcases your character and perseverance. For example, many entrepreneurs ended up navigating some very rough waters when the recession hit in 2008. That's nothing to be ashamed of and totally relatable to everyone else whose world was rocked by those tough times. Of course, pure tragedy doesn't really play well for branding purposes, because you really do need to put a positive spin on things...which brings us to our last Basic Plot...

## BASIC PLOT #7: REBIRTH

### *What's the Story?*

Rebirth is the storyline that snatches triumph from the jaws of the tragic defeat. It's Ebenezer Scrooge buying the Cratchit family a turkey on Christmas morning in "A Christmas Carol," it's the town of Bedford Falls giving Jimmy Stewart the money he needs at the end of "It's a Wonderful Life," and it's Jesus rising up on Easter morning in The Bible. Rebirth is the overcoming of overwhelming negative events or conditions in a way that gives the viewer or reader hope and inspiration.

### *How It's Used*

Look no further than the 2012 Super Bowl for a prime example of using the Rebirth paradigm to power up a brand. When Clint Eastwood walked down a dark alley to sell the comeback of Chrysler, it created such a powerful moment that the commercial became an instant political controversy. And it's not the first time Chrysler pulled off the Rebirth trick to great effect - way back in the 1980's, then-CEO Lee Iacocca promoted the brand in commercials after the car company came back from bankruptcy. Rebirth is an amazing branding storyline if you've gone through tough times and come back to success.

### *How You Can Use It*

When you're honest about your struggles, again, your audience relates. And when you can add how you triumphed over those struggles, your audience stands up and cheers like it's the end of a "Rocky" movie. This is a powerful and potent plot to use for branding, when the story fits.

So those are the seven ways you can put Story-Selling to work for you or your business. But actually, we have a little surprise for you...

There are actually *eight* ways you can use Story-Selling. And here's that extra bonus basic plot:

## BASIC PLOT #8: ALL OF THE OTHER SEVEN

As we've hinted at here and there, the best Story-Selling technique uses elements of *all* (or most) seven of the basic plots we've discussed. You'll need a little comedy to lighten the mood...a little tragedy to pump up the drama...and either a quest or a rags-to-riches element to move the story forward. A good story has a lot of different aspects to it - and the most effective Story-Selling uses all the tools in the narrative toolbox to do the best marketing job possible.

Good luck telling *your* story - and let us know if we can help!

## About Nick

An Emmy Award Winning Director and Producer, Nick Nanton, Esq., is known as the Top Agent to Celebrity Experts around the world for his role in developing and marketing business and professional experts, through personal branding, media, marketing and PR to help them gain credibility and recognition for their accomplishments. Nick is recognized as the nation's leading expert on personal branding as Fast Company Magazine's Expert Blogger on the subject and lectures regularly on the topic at major universities around the world. His book *Celebrity Branding You®* has also been used as the textbook on personal branding for University students.

The CEO of The Dicks + Nanton Celebrity Branding Agency, an international agency with more than 1000 clients in 26 countries, Nick is an award winning director, producer and songwriter who has worked on everything from large scale events to television shows with the likes of Bill Cosby, President George H.W. Bush, Brian Tracy, Michael Gerber and many more.

Nick is recognized as one of the top thought-leaders in the business world and has co-authored 16 best-selling books alongside Brian Tracy, Jack Canfield (creator of the Chicken Soup for the soul Series), Dan Kennedy, Robert Allen, Dr. Ivan Misner (Founder of BNI), Jay Conrad Levinson (Author of the Guerilla Marketing Series), Leigh Steinberg and many others, including the breakthrough hit Celebrity Branding You!®.

Nick has led the marketing and PR campaigns that have driven more than 600 authors to Best-Seller status. Nick has been seen in *USA Today, The Wall St. Journal, Newsweek, Inc. Magazine, The New York Times, Entrepreneur® Magazine, FastCompany.com*. and has appeared on ABC, NBC, CBS, and FOX television affiliates around the country, as well as on FOX News, CNN, CNBC and MSNBC speaking on subjects ranging from branding, marketing and law, to American Idol.

Nick is a member of the Florida Bar, holds a JD from the University of Florida Levin College of Law, as well as a BSBA in Finance from the University of Florida's Warrington College of Business. Nick is a voting member of The National Academy of Recording Arts & Sciences (NARAS, Home to The GRAMMYs), a member of The National Academy of Television Arts & Sciences (Home to the Emmy Awards) co-founder of the National Academy of Best-Selling Authors, an 11-time Telly Award winner, and spends his spare time working with Young Life and Downtown Credo Orlando and rooting for the Florida Gators with his wife Kristina and their three children, Brock, Bowen and Addison.

## About JW

JW Dicks, Esq. is America's foremost authority on using personal branding for business development. He has created some of the most successful brand and marketing campaigns for business and professional clients to make them the Credible Celebrity Expert in their field and build multi-million dollar businesses using their recognized status.

JW Dicks has started, bought, built, and sold a large number of businesses over his 39-year career and developed a loyal international following as a business attorney, author, speaker, consultant, and business expert's coach. He not only practices what he preaches by using his strategies to build his own businesses, he also applies those same concepts to help clients grow their business or professional practice the ways he does.

JW has been extensively quoted in such national media as *USA Today, The Wall Street Journal, Newsweek, Inc. Magazine*, Forbes.com, CNBC.Com, and Fortune Small business. His television appearances include ABC, NBC, CBS and FOX affiliate stations around the country. He is the resident branding expert for Fast Company's internationally syndicated blog and is the publisher of Celebrity Expert Insider, a monthly newsletter targeting business and brand building strategies.

JW has written over 22 books, including numerous best sellers, and has been inducted into the National Academy of Best Selling Authors. JW is married to Linda, his wife of 39 years and they have two daughters, two granddaughters and two Yorkies. JW is a 6th generation Floridian and splits time between his home in Orlando and beach house on the Florida west coast.

## About Lindsay

Lindsay Dicks helps her clients tell their stories in the online world. Being brought up around a family of marketers, but a product of Generation Y, Lindsay naturally gravitated to the new world of online marketing. Lindsay began freelance writing in 2000 and soon after launched her own PR firm that thrived by offering an in-your-face "Guaranteed PR" that was one of the first of its type in the nation.

Lindsay's new media career is centered on her philosophy that "people buy people." Her goal is to help her clients build a relationship with their prospects and customers. Once that relationship is built and they learn to trust them as the expert in their field, then they will do business with them. Lindsay also built a patent-pending process that utilizes social media marketing, content marketing and search engine optimization to create online "buzz" for her clients that helps them to convey their business and personal story. Lindsay's clientele span the entire business map and range from doctors and small business owners to Inc 500 CEOs.

Lindsay is a graduate of the University of Florida. She is the CEO of CelebritySites™, an online marketing company specializing in social media and online personal branding. Lindsay is also a multi-best-selling author including the best-selling book "*Power Principles for Success*" which she co-authored with Brian Tracy. She was also selected as one of America's PremierExperts™ and has been quoted in *Newsweek*, the *Wall Street Journal, USA Today, Inc Magazine* as well as featured on NBC, ABC, and CBS television affiliates speaking on social media, search engine optimization and making more money online. Lindsay was also recently brought on FOX 35 News as their Online Marketing Expert.

Lindsay, a national speaker, has shared the stage with some of the top speakers in the world such as Brian Tracy, Lee Milteer, Ron LeGrand, Arielle Ford, David Bullock, Brian Horn, Peter Shankman and many others. Lindsay was also a Producer on the Emmy-nominated film Jacob's Turn.

You can connect with Lindsay at:
Lindsay@CelebritySites.com
www.twitter.com/LindsayMDicks
www.facebook.com/LindsayDicks

## About Greg

Greg Rollett, the ProductPro, is a best-selling author and online marketing expert who works with authors, experts, entertainers, entrepreneurs and business owners all over the world to help them share their knowledge and change the lives and businesses of others. After creating a successful string of his own educational products, Greg began helping others in the production and marketing of their own products.

Greg is a front-runner in utilizing the power of social media, direct response marketing and customer education to drive new leads and convert those leads into long-standing customers and advocates.

Previous clients include Coca-Cola, Miller Lite, Warner Bros and Cash Money Records, as well as hundreds of entrepreneurs and small-business owners. Greg's work has been featured on FOX News, ABC, and the Daily Buzz. Greg has written for Mashable, the Huffington Post, AOL, AMEX's Open Forum and more.

Greg loves to challenge the current business environments that constrain people to working 12-hour days during the best portions of their lives. By teaching them to leverage technology and the power of information, Greg loves helping others create freedom businesses that allow them to generate income, make the world a better place and live a radically ambitious lifestyle in the process.

A former touring musician, Greg is highly sought after as a speaker, having appeared on stages with former Florida Gov. Charlie Crist, best-selling authors Chris Brogan and Nick Nanton, as well as at events such as Affiliate Summit.

If you would like to learn more about Greg and how he can help your business, please contact him directly at greg@productprosystems.com or by calling his office at 877.897.4611.

You can also download a free report on how to create your own educational products at www.productprosystems.com.